ENVISIONING A BETTER INDIA
Volume One

# ECONOMICS WITH A HUMN FACE

**WANGBA SENJAM**

INDIA • SINGAPORE • MALAYSIA

## Notion Press Media Pvt Ltd

No. 50, Chettiyar Agaram Main Road,
Vanagaram, Chennai, Tamil Nadu – 600 095

First Published by Notion Press 2021
Copyright © Wangba Senjam 2021
All Rights Reserved.

ISBN 978-1-63940-365-3

This book has been published with all efforts taken to make the material error-free after the consent of the author. However, the author and the publisher do not assume and hereby disclaim any liability to any party for any loss, damage, or disruption caused by errors or omissions, whether such errors or omissions result from negligence, accident, or any other cause.

While every effort has been made to avoid any mistake or omission, this publication is being sold on the condition and understanding that neither the author nor the publishers or printers would be liable in any manner to any person by reason of any mistake or omission in this publication or for any action taken or omitted to be taken or advice rendered or accepted on the basis of this work. For any defect in printing or binding the publishers will be liable only to replace the defective copy by another copy of this work then available.

Dedicated with the utmost love and respect to:

1. My affectionate foster mother, MEMCHANU, who was the epitome of selflessness;
2. My beloved mother, MANITOMBI, who was honesty, humility and benevolence personified; and,
3. My Gandhian father, MODHU, who was a fine combination of good sense, perseverance and simplicity, spending his entire life in *Khadi* clothing.

All of you are and will always remain alive in my heart and mind!

# CONTENTS

| | | |
|---|---|---|
| *A Brief Introduction to Envisioning a Better India* | | *vii* |
| *Preface* | | *ix* |
| *Acknowledgements* | | *xiii* |

| | | |
|---|---|---|
| Chapter One | The Faulty Conventional Concept of the Poverty Line and its Alternative | 1 |
| Chapter Two | The Strategy for Eradication of Poverty Through Intensive Development of Human Capital and Democratic Redistribution of Physical Capital | 28 |
| Chapter Three | Towards Transforming the Prison Population from Liabilities into Assets of the Nation | 69 |
| Chapter Four | Putting Gold in the Dock for Robbing Mankind | 99 |
| Chapter Five | The Extravagant Practices of Hinduism and the Concept of Economical Piety | 112 |
| Chapter Six | The Digital Anti-Speeding Code Enforcement Ecosystem and a Brief Analysis of its Economic Impact | 130 |

| | |
|---|---|
| *Appendices* | *151* |
| *Index* | *159* |

# A BRIEF INTRODUCTION TO *ENVISIONING A BETTER INDIA*

Though India is emerging on the global scene as an all-round force to be reckoned with, it still remains confronted with a host of challenging issues on almost every front, be it the economy, geopolitics, governance, justice or security. For example, on the economic front, we have the problems of massive underemployment and unemployment, exclusive economic growth and increasing income inequality with the top 10 per cent of the adult population capturing a mind-boggling 54.20 per cent of national income in 2014, according to the *World Inequality Report 2018*. In the interrelated realms of geopolitics and national security, India today stands severely pitted against an increasingly belligerent China, not to mention Pakistan, which holds a pathological grudge against India. Then there is also the overburdened judicial system, which was recently reported in the mainstream media to be sitting on a growing adjudication backlog of plus or minus 4.4 crore cases, mostly pending for years and some even for decades. These are just some of the major challenges confronting the nation at present.

Being a well-intentioned citizen with a strong sense of responsibility towards the nation and, by extension, the whole human civilization, albeit with my fair share of human weaknesses, I cannot afford, especially while sitting idle in this so-called correctional home at an estimated average daily cost of about 150

INR to the exchequer and remaining denied any way of earning my keep, to shy away from: (i) devoting myself to regular sessions of painstaking study, analysis and reflection on how to navigate and surmount some of the country's pressing issues like the ones cited above; and (ii) getting across my earnest ideas for a better India, even at the risk of being derided as a blatant endeavour to stick my oar in or even set the agenda for the nation.

I have, therefore, embarked on *Envisioning A Better India*, which is a multidisciplinary research and authorship project, intended to take the form of a series of books addressing some of the challenging issues confronting the country and also proposing some original ideas for transforming India into a model nation where the people are treated on an egalitarian footing; where the elusive inclusive economic growth becomes the norm; where it is really possible even for the poorest of the poor to pursue justice meaningfully and effectively enough; and where harmony, stability and prosperity flow like the Ganges.

Let me conclude this introduction here with my firm commitment to give a hundred per cent to this project, which I am in for the long haul.

**WANGBA SENJAM**

# PREFACE

*Economics with A Human Face* is the first book to have been completed under the *Envisioning A Better India* project. As you go through each chapter of the book, you observe my insights and ideas gradually crystallizing into some radical concepts about, and answers to, the given issues. However, it is the country's chronic poverty that I have treated quite extensively in the book, with the first two chapters revolving only around it. Because this intractable issue left an indelible mark on my life and has, therefore, always attracted my utmost attention.

From my point of view, poverty in India is nothing short of a socio-economic prison wherein millions of households continue to languish for their 'unforgivable crime' of having no dependable means of overcoming it on their own, thanks to the protracted failure of the country's successive governments in the last 74 years of independence to give the poor what is their due by virtue of being citizens of the country. Indeed, the poor have always been treated unjustly, albeit tacitly, as a colossal burden on the nation that has to be dragged along only with the aid of limited employment guarantee schemes and food and fuel subsidies.

What is pretty conspicuous by its prolonged absence in the country is a coherent anti-poverty policy that is based on democratically sound economics. Our so-called poverty alleviation programmes like the IRDP(1978), NREGA(2005), NRLM(2011), and NFSA(2013) can, at best, be effective in providing the poor with a means of keeping the wolf from the door, which is, of course, the minimum that the government can afford to assure them. Because empty stomachs, if caused to remain so for long, will naturally get filled up with a potentially destructive cocktail of disenchantment with, and a desire for rebellion against, the powers that be. But preventing hunger cannot, by any stretch of the imagination, be equated with empowering the poor to come out of the harsh prison of poverty.

This book is made up of six chapters, with the first one, *The Faulty Conventional Concept of the Poverty Line and its Alternative*, finding fault with the conventional concept of the poverty line and also offering an alternative model for determining poverty. Chapter Two, *The Strategy for Eradication of Poverty through Intensive Development of Human Capital and Democratic Redistribution of Physical Capital*, puts forward a strategy for the country to seamlessly build the poor population into its economic process by skilling and giving them the wherewithal and opportunity to embark on an economically meaningful and productive journey and ultimately free themselves from the prison of poverty by means of their own skill and labour. Chapter Three, *Towards Transforming the Prison Population from Liabilities into Assets of the Nation*, explains why and how reformation of the prison population must be actively pursued and their massive economic potential efficiently tapped for the good of the nation as a whole. Chapter Four, *Putting Gold in the Dock for Robbing Mankind*, shows the regressive aspects of the worldwide accumulation and aggrandisement of gold and also highlights, albeit briefly, some important realities associated with the yellow metal in India. Chapter Five, *The Extravagant Practices of Hinduism and the Concept of Economical Piety*, highlights the extravagant aspects of Hinduism and introduces the concept of economical piety. Last but not least, Chapter Six, *Digital Anti-Speeding Code Enforcement Ecosystem and A Brief Analysis of Its Economic Impact*, proposes a digital framework for putting an effective brake on speeding, which is not only the biggest cause of motor accidents, being solely responsible for the vast majority of all road casualties, but also makes a significant dent in the Indian economy. It also offers a brief assessment of the digital framework's general economic impact at the end.

As the book has been written in the face of all the peculiar obstacles of imprisonment such as my inability to access the internet for statistical updates, reference papers, etc., stressful spells and distracting surroundings, I may not be off the mark to suggest that the subject matter of the book still has some scope for further elaboration and refinement, which, I think, will be possible only with more data and in an environment that is conducive to deep study, analysis and reflection.

But then again, I am reasonably hopeful that the radical concepts and proposed answers to the given issues, however imperfect they may be, or at least the humanitarian feelings and logic embodied therein, will not fail to appeal to your conscience and sense of socio-economic justice, especially if you make it a joint effort of your head and heart to peruse this book.

**WANGBA SENJAM**

# ACKNOWLEDGEMENTS

It is very satisfying indeed to have completed my first book in the form of *Economics With A Human Face* under the *Envisioning A Better India* project. The authorship and publication of this book would not have been possible but for the valuable support that I have been fortunate enough to receive from my special friends, viz.:

1. Ms. Nabenita Tongbram (MTech), an Executive Officer (Environment) in a subsidiary under the Ministry of Coal, Government of India, who provided me every now and then with valuable resources such as statistical inputs, reference books and important feedback, not to mention her words of encouragement and expression of confidence in my academic faculty and potential.

2. Ch. Yaikhomba Singh, a major in the Indian Army, who is more of a younger brother than a friend and never failed to oblige me with whatever reference data, articles and books that I had asked him for.

3. Miss S. Sangeeta Devi (a young entrepreneur), Mr Utpal Dutta (Advocate) and Miss Smriti Sharma (Advocate), who proved to be of great help by running some important errands for me towards finishing this book.

4. Those friends from Manipur, Assam, Himachal Pradesh and West Bengal who helped me out with important price data, with some of them even taking the trouble to survey

small random samples of grocers and road-side vegetable vendors in their respective areas to gather price data.

5. Mrs. Abha Garg, who undertook the job of typing more than half the manuscript, including the flowcharts.

6. Mr. Gautam Mali, Welfare Officer of Presidency Correctional Home, Kolkata (West Bengal) and, by extension, Superintendent thereof, who allowed me to type up a major portion of the book in one of the Welfare Office computers during my confinement therein.

7. Dr. Kh. Lakshmi (MBBS, MS), whose evaluative comments on the DACE Ecosystem instilled into me a reasonable amount of confidence to include it in this book as one of its chapters.

8. Last but not least, Notion Press Team, especially Ms. Urmi, Ms. Nikitha, Ms. Christina and my publishing managers Ms. Padmavathi Rajaram and Ms. Sai Swasthika, who provided me with commendably professional support towards the publication of this book and undertook the uphill task of creating a long-term bridge between this book and its audience.

Indeed, I am and will always remain profoundly indebted to them all. May health and happiness be with them and their families!

**WANGBA SENJAM**

# Chapter One

# THE FAULTY CONVENTIONAL CONCEPT OF THE POVERTY LINE AND ITS ALTERNATIVE

"In India, as in other poor countries, we have a line that is invisible and abstract and yet more powerful and pervasive than anything the West or the Japanese have invented. It is called the poverty line. Above the poverty line are three meals a day. Below it is a spectrum that stretches all the way from 2.99 to zero meals. As familiar as a clothes-line, most people in India spend their entire lives trying to reach out beyond it. It is their greatest aspiration. If you are fortunate, if the gods smile and you are lucky, you may get a glimpse of it. You can't see the line, you can't touch it, and five hundred million people are trying to get to it."

Kiran Nagarkar, *Ravan & Eddie*

Poverty is usually defined as the inability to meet a minimum level of consumption or the state of living below the poverty line, which is expressed in terms of how much money is needed to meet the minimum level of consumption. Poverty can also be understood in absolute and relative terms. Absolute poverty is the inability to afford a fixed minimum level of consumption that is independent of time or place, whereas relative poverty is the lack of resources to participate in the customary activities of a given society at a given time. Those people who are unable to afford the fixed minimum level of consumption or take part in the customary activities of society are categorized as the poor. So how is the minimum level of consumption or the poverty line determined?

International organizations and researchers dealing with socio-economic matters mostly arrive at their respective USD-denominated international poverty lines on the basis of prices vis-à-vis a set of goods typically consumed by the poor or even by averaging the official poverty lines of all or a given set of poor countries, adjusted for the purchasing power parity (PPP) with the USD, conveniently neglecting the deviations of national poverty lines. In May 2014, the World Bank, which has reviewed its definition of poverty and methodology of calculating its international poverty line from time to time, proposed 1.78 USD per day on 2011 PPP basis as the so-called international poverty line, only to revise it upwards to 1.90 USD per day with a PPP value of 32.52 INR in October 2015.

It is a standard practice for the state to set up expert committees to study poverty and estimate its extent from time to time. Since its independence in 1947, India has seen several such committees, which must have crunched a great deal of data, particularly NSS and NAS, before deciding on their respective poverty lines and estimates. But interestingly enough, their poverty lines and estimates vary significantly. Without going very far back, if two such committees may be referred to, we have the so-called Tendulkar Committee and its successor, the Rangarajan Committee. According to the former, 29.6% of the Indian population or 354 million Indians lived below the poverty line in 2009–10, but it fell to 21.9% or 269 million Indians in 2011–12. The Tendulkar Committee based these estimates on its poverty lines of 33 INR for urban areas and 27 INR for rural areas. However, in June 2014, the Rangarajan Committee came up with its own poverty lines of 47 INR and

32 INR for urban and rural areas respectively on the basis of which the percentages of the Indian population living in poverty in 2009–2010 and 2011–12 were revised at 38.2%, i.e. about 454 million Indians and 29.5% or approximately 363 million Indians respectively.

The differences between the poverty lines of the two committees in question are the obvious explanation for the discrepancies in their poverty estimates. But the question is, how and why did they arrive at significantly different poverty lines in the first place? Though the answer is to be found mainly in their methodological differences and also data imperfection exemplified by the growing divergence between the NSS and NAS consumption aggregates as highlighted in several studies[1], it is not within the scope of this paper to dissect them.

Going by the higher poverty lines, set by the Rangarajan Committee, if you live on any amount under 47 INR per day in an urban area or 32 INR per day in a rural area, you will be counted poor. But if you manage to live on 47 INR or above per day in an urban area and 32 INR or above per day in a rural area, you will be counted out of poverty. It may be quite intriguing to see the wide difference of 15 INR between the urban and rural poverty lines. One major reason for this wide difference is the common perception that the cost of living

---

1. (a) Martin Ravallion (2000), "Should Poverty Measures Be Anchored to the National Accounts?", Economic and Political Weekly, 34:3245–52;

   (b) Central Statistical Organisation (2008), Report of the Group for Examining Discrepancy in PFCE Estimates from the NSSO Consumer Expenditure Data and Estimates, compiled by National Accounts Division (Ministry of Statistics and Programme Implementation, Government of India; and,

   (c) Sundaram and Suresh Tendulkar (2001), "NAS-NSS Estimates of Private Consumption for Poverty Estimation: A Disaggregated Comparison for 1993–94, Economic and Political Weekly, 42(30): 119–129.

is relatively high in urban areas, where even water has to be bought in many cases, whereas households in rural areas mostly enjoy some significant advantages over urban counterparts like easier and free access to water, being able to buy some types of food produce directly from the farm and local grower-vendors at lower prices and so on. Many rural households also keep free-range fowl and cattle. Yet many more of them grow vegetables in whatever vacant land they own. But not all rural households are fortunate enough to be able to keep fowl and cattle or own any land apart from whatever is occupied by their dwellings. In some rural areas people can even go hunting and fishing and collect edible plants, fungi, roots, etc. in the wild so as to supplement their food requirements. However, in many other respects, the rural populace is in a comparatively disadvantageous position. For instance, the rural grocer incurs a higher transport cost than his urban counterpart – the farther away from the wholesaler, the higher the cost of transporting goods. Though the rural grocer may well be bound by trade regulations not to sell products above their printed maximum retail prices, he is, of course, at liberty to sell loose commodities, say a bag of rice and a tin of mustard oil, at higher prices per unit. So it is quite natural for the rural grocer to pass the burden of the higher cost of transport on to his customers by charging more per unit of commodities sold than his urban counterpart charges urban customers or he would if he did not incur the high cost of transport.

Moreover, referring to the All India Consumer Price Index numbers (new series), the rural CPI (NS) actuals have always been higher than their urban cousins. In April 2016, the rural CPI (NS) number stood at 129.0 and its urban counterpart at 125.5 with 2010 and 2012 being equal to 100. The corresponding figures of April 2017 were 132.9 and 129.1 respectively. So the CPI (NS) numbers also categorically testify to the fact that the rural populace faces a consistently higher price situation, especially in terms of processed commodities.

It is claimed that the minimum per capita requirement of calories is 2,400 calories per day in rural areas and 2,100 calories per day in urban areas. The logic behind this claim is that the rural workforce is mostly engaged in physically more demanding work than urban workers. However, it can no longer be sustained primarily because of the increasing mechanization of agriculture, in which the vast majority of the rural workforce are employed and the employment of urban workers in automobile workshops, general construction, operation of heavy machinery, etc., which demand heavy manual labour. Also, the calorific requirements of individuals engaged in a particular activity vary according to their weights. For example, driving demands about 204 calories per hour for a 58-kg person but about 228 calories per hour for a 65-kg person. So it may be stated that the rural-urban difference in terms of calorific requirements is actually more a myth than a reality. As a matter of fact, the NSSO report on employment says that the actual number of hours worked per week on average is 53–54 hours in urban areas and 46–47 hours in rural areas. In its November report[2], an expert group – the so-called Suresh Tendulkar Committee – set up by the Planning Commission recommended, inter alia, moving away from basing the poverty lines on calorific norms because of the poor correlation between calorie consumption and nutritional outcome.

In the light of the above and other relevant facts, I feel compelled to conclude that the wide difference between the urban and rural poverty lines is a proof that they do not reflect reality and must, therefore, be debated so as to arrive at more convincing and realistic poverty lines if the country has to stick to the concept of the poverty line as the basis for determining whether a person is poor or not and estimating the extent of poverty.

---

2. Report of the Expert Group to Review the Methodology for Estimation of Poverty, Planning Commission, Government of India, 2009. (*http://planningcommission.nic.in/reports/genrep/rep_pov.pdf*)

Now, coming back to the poverty lines, let us examine how realistic it is to use them in determining who is poor and who is not. For this purpose, let me take the hypothetical case of a five-member household consisting of Tomba, his father, mother, wife and son aged 34, 56, 55, 33 and 12 years respectively. So beginning with food requirements, let me present in tabular form the household's minimum daily diet required to stay healthy enough to carry on normal day-to-day life.

### Table 1.1: Tea-Bread Breakfast

| Sl. No. | Item | Quantity | Approximate Calories | Price in INR Rural | Price in INR Urban |
|---|---|---|---|---|---|
| 1 | Sugar | 75g | 290 | 5 | 4.20 |
| 2 | Tea | 12.5g | 2 | 5^ | 5^ |
| 3 | White Bread | 300g | 681 | 21^ | 21^ |
| 4 | Milk Powder | 22g | 90 | 9.40^ | 9.40^ |
| 5 | LPG* | 35g | NA | 1.54$ | 1.54$ |
|  | TOTAL | NA | 1063 | 41.94 | 41.14 |

Table 1 shows what it takes to prepare the most basic form of breakfast, consisting of tea and sliced bread, which costs Tomba's household 41.94 INR (rural) or 41.14 INR (urban). Presuming price constancy, the annual cost of breakfast for Tomba's household is 16,108.90 INR (rural) or 15,816.90 INR (urban). In terms of calories, this form of breakfast gives Tomba's

---

^ Based on the average of MRP's of at least two brands.

* Some poor households may be located in the proximity of wooded forest from where they can collect tinder to use as or supplement cooking fuels. But there are many other poor households that depend entirely on purchased fuels, particularly LPG, for cooking. Moreover, the *Pradhan Mantri Ujjwala Yojana* has provided millions of poor households with LPG connections. So the cost of LPG consumption has been estimated and incorporated into the diet-related tables.

$ Government Rate (Subsidized).

household an optimum amount of 1063 calories or 212.6 calories per head.

Table 1.2: Two-Course/*Dal-Chawal* Lunch

| Sl. No. | Item | Quantity | Approximate Calories | Price in INR | |
|---|---|---|---|---|---|
| | | | | Rural | Urban |
| 1 | White Rice (low-quality) | 1.25kg | 4075 | 28 | 27 |
| 2 | Pulses | 375g | 1095 | 26.35 | 26 |
| 3 | Mustard Oil | 35ml | 315 | 5^ | 5^ |
| 4 | Onion | 75g | 30 | 2 | 1.80 |
| 5 | Garlic | 15g | 22 | 1.10 | 1.07 |
| 6 | Ginger | 15g | 12 | 1.22 | 1.35 |
| 7 | Turmeric | 2.5g | 9 | 1.25^ | 1.25^ |
| 8 | Green Chilli | 20g | 8 | 0.80 | 0.84 |
| 9 | Iodine Salt | 25g | 0 | 0.50^ | 0.50^ |
| 10 | Citrus Fruit | 50g | 21 | 2.80 | 3.20 |
| 11 | LPG* | 210g | NA | 9$ | 9$ |
| | TOTAL | NA | 5587 | 78.02 | 77.01 |

As we can see in Table 1.2, it costs Tomba's household 78.02 INR (rural) or 77.01 (urban) to prepare a two-course lunch, or more precisely, *dal-chawal* of 5,587 calories for the household or

---

NB: The price of each item, barring pulses and vegetables, is the average of the varying prices of the same item collected in July and August 2018 from a small random sample of grocers, roadside vendors and poor households in Manipur, Assam, West Bengal and Himachal Pradesh. However, the given prices of pulses and vegetables (Tables 1.2 and 1.3) were arrived at by means of double-averaging, that is, first averaging the varying prices of each item in two separate baskets of pulses ( lentils, chickpeas, moong, lobia, tur and urad) and vegetables ( cabbage, cauliflower, mustard greens, potato, marrow, aubergine and okra), which are typically consumed by the poor, collected through the same survey and then averaging the resulting average prices of the items in the two baskets separately.

1117.40 calories per head. For the whole year or 365 days, the amount required is 28,477.30 INR (rural) or 28,108.65 INR (urban). Adjusting for the per capita entitlement of 5 Kg of rice per month at 3 INR per kg under the National Food Security Act, 2013, the annual cost of *dal-chawal* for Tomba's household comes down to 22,657.30 INR (rural) or 22,528.65 INR (urban).

Table 1.3: Two-Course/*Roti-Sabji* Supper

| Sl. No. | Item | Quantity | Approximate Calories | Price in INR | |
|---|---|---|---|---|---|
| | | | | Rural | Urban |
| 1 | Wheat Flour | 1.25kg | 4550 | 36 | 34 |
| 2 | Vegetables | 1kg | 845 | 14 | 16 |
| 3 | Mustard Oil | 35ml | 315 | 5^ | 5^ |
| 4 | Onion | 75g | 30 | 2 | 1.80 |
| 5 | Garlic | 15g | 22 | 1.10 | 1.07 |
| 6 | Ginger | 15g | 12 | 1.22 | 1.35 |
| 7 | Turmeric | 2.5g | 9 | 1.25^ | 1.25^ |
| 8 | Green Chilli | 20g | 8 | 0.80 | 0.84 |
| 9 | Iodine Salt | 25g | 0 | 0.50^ | 0.50^ |
| 10 | LPG* | 219 | NA | 9.36$ | 9.36$ |
| | TOTAL | NA | 5791 | 71.23 | 71.17 |

As shown in Table 1.3, a modest two-course supper – *roti-sabji* – for Tomba's household can be prepared at a cost of 71.23 INR (rural) or 71.17 INR (urban). So assuming price constancy, the annual cost of *roti-sabji* to Tomba's household is 25,998.95 INR (rural) or 25,976.05 INR (urban). A question may well arise here: If a two-course meal (supper) carrying a total of 5,791 calories for the household or 1,158.20 calories per head can be prepared at a cost of 71.23 INR (rural) or 71.17 INR (urban), why should Tomba's household prepare another two-course meal (lunch) with a total calorific content of 5,587 calories for the household or 1,117.40 calories per head at a higher cost of 78.02 INR (rural) or 77.01 INR (urban)? The answer lies in the differences between the two meals in terms of composition. The two-course supper is loaded with energy and fibre, whereas the two-course lunch contains proteins and vitamins, which are also essential for health.

So the total amount of calories that Tomba's household can optimally derive from the tea-bread breakfast, *dal-chawal* lunch and *roti-sabji* supper is 12,441 calories or 2,488.20 calories per head, which is 88.20 calories (rural) or 388.20 calories (urban) more than the per capita calorie requirements, as estimated by the World Bank. If the loss of food items in dressing and preparing is taken into account, the excess calories will just vanish, at least in the rural case.

Moving on to the non-food requirements of Tomba's household, let me classify them into two categories – miscellaneous monthly and yearly requirements – and present them in the form of two separate tables for presentational convenience.

**Table 1.4: Miscellaneous Monthly Requirements**

| Sl. No. | Item | | Quantity | Cost in INR |
|---|---|---|---|---|
| 1 | Toilet Soap | | 1.50kg | 150^ |
| 2 | Toothpaste | | 375g | 150^ |
| 3 | Detergent Powder/Bar | | 1kg | 100^ |
| 4 | Dishwash Bar | | 800g | 80^ |
| 5 | Hair Oil | | 300ml | 120^ |
| 6 | Sanitary Towel | | 10 | 45^ |
| 7 | Personal Grooming (Male) | Haircut for Males | 3 | 60 |
|   |   | Shaving Blade for adult Males | 2 | 20^ |
|   | TOTAL | | NA | 725 |

As all items in Table 1.4 come in packaged form with printed MRP's, except Personal Grooming, the question of rural-urban price differentials does not arise under normal circumstances. So Tomba's household, whether located in a rural or urban area, is presumed to spend 725 INR per month or 8,700 INR per year on miscellaneous monthly requirements.

**Table 1.5: Miscellaneous Yearly Requirements**

| Sl. No. | Item | | Quantity | Estimated Cost In INR |
|---|---|---|---|---|
| 1 | Replacement (R)/Wear & Tear (W&T) Cost of Clothing | Underwear (R) | 8+9+1=18 Sets | 2,160 |
| | | Daywear (R) | 8+1=9 Sets | 6,300 |
| | | Towel (R) | 10 Pieces | 500 |
| | | Bedding (W&T) | NA | 1,500 |
| | | Shoe (R) | 2+2=4 Pairs | 1,600 |
| | | Slipper (R) | 5×3=15 Pairs | 1,500 |
| 2 | Education of Tomba's 12-year-old Son at a Govt. School | Admission and Other Fees | NA | Free under the RTE Act |
| | | Books and Other Study Items | NA | 1,200 |
| | | Uniform | 1 Set | 2,100 |
| 3 | Treatment of Minor Seasonal Health Problems like Influenza and Cold | | NA | 500 |
| 4 | Transport | | NA | 3,500 |
| 5 | Power Consumption for Lighting | | 600kWh | 2,400 |
| 6 | Toothbrush | | 2×5=10 | 200 |
| 7 | Contingencies@ | | NA | 1,500 |

@ Contingencies are: a bulb may fuse; part of dwelling may be damaged in the wind, hailstorm, etc.; a household item may be broken or stolen; and, so on.

| Sl. No. | Item | Quantity | Estimated Cost In INR |
|---|---|---|---|
| 8 | Wear and Tear Cost of Household Goods | NA | 2,000 |
|  | ESTIMATED TOTAL | NA | 26,960 |

Table 1.5 shows the miscellaneous requirements of Tomba's household, whose cost is best calculated on a yearly basis and has been done so, resulting in an estimated total cost of 26,960 INR per annum.

Adding up the estimated yearly costs of all basic requirements of Tomba's household, shown in the tables above, I find the annual total cost of a basic living for Tomba's household to be 1,00,425.15 INR (rural) or 99,981.60 INR (urban). As water, especially potable water, is commonly bought from private and public water supply agencies in most if not all urban areas, the yearly cost of water consumption, working out at 4,800 INR[+] for a five-member urban household, has to be taken into account. So the annual cost

---

[+] A random sample of poor households in certain urban conurbations of Manipur, Assam, West Bengal and Himachal Pradesh was surveyed in July and August 2018 as regards their expenditure on water. Though some of the poor households surveyed claim that they do not have to buy water and can manage it somehow throughout the year, 8+ out of 10 claim that they have to buy water sometimes if not always, with their expenditure claims varying widely. For example, one household at Chakkar, an urban area in Shimla (Himachal Pradesh), claims that it spends about 7,200 INR per year on direct purchase of water, excluding the pumping cost. But another household at Naoremthong, an urban conurbation of Imphal West (Manipur), says that it spends about 2,500 INR per annum on buying drinking water, especially to compensate for short supply of water in the summer. In order to arrive at the yearly cost of water consumption, I add up the numbers of members of all households surveyed and the resulting total is divided by 5, the given strength of Tomba's household. The quotient is then used to divide the aggregate yearly expenditure of those poor households claiming to have to buy water, thus coming up with the amount of 4,800 INR as the annual cost of water for a poor urban household of five members.

of a basic living for Tomba's household in an urban area is revised upwards at 1,04,781.60 INR at 2018 prices.

On the other hand, going by the poverty lines of 32 INR (rural) and 47 INR (urban), set by the Rangarajan Committee in 2014, the calculated yearly poverty lines[++] of Tomba's household work out at 58,400 INR (rural) and 85,765 INR (urban). Linking these yearly poverty lines to their appropriate CPI (NS) numbers increases them to 67,416.96 INR (rural) and 96,560.81 INR (urban) in 2017–18. However, even the CPI (NS)-linked calculated yearly poverty lines fall short of the corresponding annual costs of a basic living for Tomba's household by 33,008.23 INR or 32.87% in the rural case and 8,220.79 INR or 7.87% in the urban case. Given the fact that even 32 INR and 47 INR are definitely not enough to serve as rural and urban poverty lines respectively, it is quite easy to conclude that the poverty estimates based on the lower officially accepted poverty lines of 27 INR (rural) and 33 INR (urban), set by the so-called Tendulkar Committee, are nothing but a gross underestimation of the actual extent of poverty in India!

It is now crystal clear that the per diem poverty lines of 32 INR (rural) per person in 2014–15 or 36.94 INR (rural) per person in 2017–18 and ) and 47 INR (urban) per person in 2014–15 or 52.91 INR (urban) in 2017–18 are not sufficient to meet the requirements of even a very basic living, let alone be the line determining whether a person is poor or not. So if compelled to actually live on either, Tomba's household or any other household, for that matter, will have no option but

---

++ Take a poverty line, say 32 INR, and multiply it by the number of household members, which is 5 in Tomba's case. What you now get is 160 INR, which is the per diem poverty line of Tomba's household. To arrive at the yearly rural poverty line of Tomba's household, simply multiply 160 INR by the number of days in a non-leap year, i.e. 365, and you get 58,400 INR, which is the yearly rural poverty line of Tomba's household or any other 5-member household.

to cut down on or altogether forgo some of the very basic items given in the tables above. But the question is, what else should Tomba's household be expected to cut down on or forgo as many basic requirements of life by today's normal social standards such as fish, meat, mobile phone and basic forms of home entertainment like radio and TV are forgone already? Should it be expected to switch from toothpaste and toothbrush to powdered charcoal and chewing stick? Should Tomba's son be made to give up education? Should it go back to the primitive method of doing the dishes with ash or sand? Should it scale back its overall food consumption, which is already minimal and barely enough in terms of calories, vitamins, proteins and other essentials? Should Tomba's wife forgo sanitary towel, which is essential for her physical well-being? Should the male members forgo haircut and shaving? Or assuming its proximity to and expansive pasture and/or wooded forest, should it choose to go collecting cow dung and/or tinder to use as cooking fuel so as to cut back on or entirely forgo LPG/kerosene consumption?

Rhetorical as those questions may be, treating them with a little imagination will help picture the possible conditions of Tomba's household if it actually has to subsist on the those poverty lines. Indeed, those poverty lines are a gross under-calculation of the ever-increasing cost of living at best or perhaps a weak attempt on the part of the expert committee concerned to strike a balance between bringing the actual extent of poverty in India to the fore and doing the people in power a calculated favour by sympathizing with their political compulsion to systematically underreport poverty in the country and conceal the failure or ineffectiveness of India's corruption-ridden anti-poverty measures from the common people and the Opposition and, by extension, the world.

In the socio-economic context of India today, if there is any kind of living that either of the poverty lines can ensure, it is only what may be aptly called 'primitive existence'. In other words, the so-called poverty lines of India are in reality nothing more than a hollow euphemism for the primitive existence line, living on which unavoidably means surviving under primitive conditions in this day and age, wherein autonomous vehicles, quantum computing and cloning have become realities!

The shortfall in the poverty lines is not the only problem in the process of estimating poverty in India. Other problems like the diverse realities of Indian households and methodological imperfections also affect the analysis and measurement of poverty significantly. So if the intent is to more meaningfully analyse and estimate poverty in India, either these problems must be addressed properly or a new alternative mechanism for determining more pragmatically whether a person or household is poor or not and estimating the extent of poverty and bringing out its real nature must be devised so that the destructive phenomenon of poverty can be handled more effectively with the aid of more accurate data on and insights into it. To me the latter option, that is, to devise a new alternative mechanism, looks more appealing and easier.

## THE ALTERNATIVE MECHANISM

When it comes to the measurement of poverty, a bone of contention always arises between two groups of economists as to whether poverty should be estimated in absolute or relative terms. The group following the absolute school of thought argues that the measurement of poverty should be based on a fixed minimum level of consumption independent of time or place, which is just enough to stay healthy and ensure limited housing and minimum clothing. However, the relative school of thought construes poverty as the inability to afford the average standards of living in a given society at a given time. If the former prevails, technical progress and steady rise in income will ultimately resolve the intractable problem of poverty. But if the latter is followed, it becomes by far more difficult to lift poor people above the poverty line. Moreover, the extent of relative poverty is higher than that of absolute poverty, thereby magnifying the challenge of poverty in the former case.

The perennial clash between the absolute and relative schools of thought may happen mainly on an academic level. But it certainly has implications for domain policy makers across the world. Indeed, the failure of the global community of economists to come up with a single consensual concept of poverty and the poverty line leaves people responsible for dealing with the issue of poverty, particularly policy makers and their political bosses, a great deal of liberty to interpret poverty in whatever way suits them most.

In the case of India, it is the absolute concept of poverty and the poverty line that has found currency among domain policy makers and, therefore, been in application for the official analysis and measurement of poverty. Even in absolute terms, the extent of poverty in India is very high. So it is quite conceivable how high the incidence of relative poverty in India must be.

Even if both the absolute and relative concepts of poverty and the poverty line have also been in widespread currency among social scientist, particularly among economists, neither cannot be a definitive concept per se. As far as I can understand, the absolute concept of poverty and the poverty line naturally means understating poverty; whereas following the relative one will necessarily result in the overestimation of poverty. In either case, the planning and implementation of anti-poverty measures and allocation of resources thereto are bound to be significantly affected. So a more realistic concept of poverty and the poverty line to serve as a new alternative mechanism for deciding whether a person/household is poor or not and estimating the extent of poverty in an area or community has to be ideated and formulated by striking a balance between the absolute and relative concepts of poverty and the poverty line.

For the purpose of finding a middle way between the absolute and relative concepts of poverty and the poverty line, I have not only borrowed and slightly modified the three traditional criteria basically associated with the former but also formulated six new criteria, which are elaborated below:

1. Being able to afford food that is sufficient in terms of quality, quantity and variety to stay healthy enough to carry on normal day-to-day activities.

2. Owning a dwelling of at least semi-*pucca* standards with a toilet and access to the electricity supply or a solar power installation.

3. Possession of at least the bare minimum of clothing.

   These are the slightly modified versions of the three traditional criteria used for fixing the absolute poverty line.

4. Proper education up to at least the age of 18 years. Because it is only through proper education that one can so attain a minimum level of intellectual capacity as to be able to strive for an adequately productive and successful life in this increasingly competitive world.

5. Being able to afford the bare necessities of personal hygiene such as toiletries, shaving kit and sanitary towel.

6. Savings/cash in reserve of at least 5,000 INR for meeting the cost of miscellaneous ordinary contingencies such as replacement of a fused bulb and purchase of some medicine for a minor health problem.

7. Having an individual/joint bank account in the name of one or more of household members. Apart from being the principal criterion for financial inclusion, a bank account plays a significant role in the life of a person or household by facilitating access to credit and receipt of state welfare benefits, and offering a range of facilities such as ATM

card and chequebook. So it is of great importance for every household to open at least one bank account and get formally included in the financial system.

8. Owning a mobile phone, which is a generally available affordable medium of communication. Unquestionably a great technological game changer, the mobile phone has come to be adopted as a convenient means of identification, authentication and authorization in many areas, including banking and implementation of social welfare programmes. So it is imperative for every household to own at least one mobile phone, which will have an empowering impact on it.

9. Lastly, owning a TV set, which is not only a basic form of entertainment but also an effective medium of educating and empowering the masses by constantly supplying them with critical information on a wide range of subjects such as current affairs, health, sanitation, agriculture, constitutional rights, laws and social welfare programmes.

These nine criteria (hereafter referred to as 'the $3_{TC}+6_{NC}$ set' as a shorthand) together form the basis for my conception of the line of demarcation between being in and out of poverty. Only when a household actually fulfils the entire $3_{TC}+6_{NC}$ set or otherwise attains the net financial capacity to fulfill it by dint of income from employment/self-employment and/or government assistance via social welfare schemes like the *Jan Dhan Yojana, Pradhan Mantri Awaas Yojana and Ayushman Bharat Yojana,* and laws like the Right to Education Act, 2009 and National Food Security Act, 2013, must it be counted out of poverty. But if the household fails to fulfill the $3_{TC}+6_{NC}$ set or attain the net financial capacity to fulfill the same, then it must be registered as a poor household.

It is now clear that my conception of the dividing line between a poor household and a non-poor one is broader than the absolute concept of the poverty line by virtue of the incorporation of the six new criteria, i.e. $6_{NC}$, over and above the three traditional criteria, i.e. $3_{TC}$, on which the absolute poverty line is based. Moreover, the fact that the former makes allowance for some present-day necessities – remember those criteria involving a bank account, mobile phone and TV set – is contrary to the latter being independent of time, notwithstanding both being independent of place, meaning that both are as applicable to an Indian household as to a Venezuelan or Jamaican counterpart, irrespective of ethnicity, religion, polity, etc.

However, being broader than the absolute concept of the poverty line does not necessarily qualify my conception of the dividing line between the poor and the non-poor to be treated as the relative concept of the poverty line or an approximate version thereof. As already noted, it can be applied independently of place, whereas the relative concept of the poverty line is applicable solely to a given society at a given time. Further, the fulfillment of the $3_{TC}+6_{NC}$ set is by no means sufficient to be translated as living as per the average standards of any particular society or participation in the customary activities of society, a condition fundamental to the relative concept of the poverty line.

So it may now be concluded that altogether my conception of the line of demarcation between the poor and the non-poor is broader than the absolute concept of the poverty line but narrower than the relative one. In other words, it strikes a balance between the two conventional concepts of the poverty line and is, therefore, a more balanced alternative mechanism for deciding whether a person/household is in or out of poverty and measuring the extent of poverty in an area or community.

Indeed, the fulfillment of the $3_{TC}+6_{NC}$ set represents a significant milestone in the life of a poor household from where it can strive in earnest to build up its socio-economic competitiveness and embark on an upward socio-economic trajectory by virtue of good health, safe living environment, basic level of intellectual capacity, higher level of socio-economic consciousness and overall empowerment flowing therefrom.

However, some questions may arise as to the possible mismatches between the $3_{TC}+6_{NC}$ set and the actual conditions and preferences of households in the real world. For example, what if a household owns an x rather than a TV set even if it meets all the other criteria of the $3_{TC}+6_{NC}$ set? What about another household that prefers a rechargeable lamp to a mobile phone, despite their price parity? What if yet another household does not own a dwelling and so lives in a rented accommodation, though it not only meets the rest of the $3_{TC}+6_{NC}$ set but also has 2 lakh INR in savings? What about those households spending significantly higher than the minimum on one criterion, say food, but lower than the minimum on another, say toiletries, though a balanced spending would have ensured the fulfillment of both the criteria in question? And so on.

Though these questions are all variations on the same theme, they all need to be answered for the sake of greater clarity. The answer to the first question has to be in the form of three conditional cases. First, if the x, which can be a piece of land, sewing machine, bicycle, etc. is meant for household use only, contributing zero to the household's income, and the current value of the x is equal to or above the current price of a low-end TV set, it must be counted out of poverty for the simple reason that it can sell the x and buy a TV set with the proceeds from its sale. Second, if the household employs the x to generate supplementary income minus which its total income falls short of the minimum level of income required to meet any other one of the $3_{TC}+6_{NC}$ set and the current value of the x is equal to or only insignificantly higher than the current price of a low-end TV set, then it has to be treated as a poor household, because selling the x to buy a TV set will create a deficit in the household's total income required to fulfill the rest of the $3_{TC}+6_{NC}$ set. The third conditional case is , if the current value of the x is in significant excess of the current price of a low-end TV set and the excess part can be reinvested in accord with the household's current human capital in something at least as productive and rewarding as the x so that the returns therefrom can compensate for the deficit in the household's total income that will arise from the sale of the x, the household must be counted out of poverty, no matter whether it retains or sells the x.

Moving on to the second question, if the household prefers a rechargeable lamp to a mobile phone, their price parity notwithstanding, it may most probably be because of factors such as lack of knowledge about the relative advantage or utility of the two items and high frequency of load-shedding or blackouts in its area. So regardless of its preference for the rechargeable lamp, the household has to be counted out of poverty, provided that apart from being able to afford either of the two items in question, it also fulfils the rest of the $3_{TC}+6_{NC}$ set.

As far as the third question is concerned, if the amount of the household's savings is sufficient to buy a parcel in a habitable area that is reachable by public transport within an hour from its present rental accommodation – this condition is important because relocation too far away can render its present socio-economic network difficult to maintain, affect its way of living and so on – and build a semi-*pucca* dwelling that is large enough to properly accommodate the entire household, then it must be counted non-poor, whether it continues to live in the rented accommodation or not. But if the amount of its savings is not enough for that, it has to be categorized as a household in poverty. Because without the household owning a dwelling of at least semi-*pucca* standards or having attained the financial capacity to buy one such dwelling or a parcel and build one, it can be said to have no real control over its own shelter, which is one of the few indisputable conditions of poverty.

The answer to the last question lies in one common presumption that most if not all households have some sense of priority and proportion, though this may well be an oversimplification of an answer to it. Indeed, the households in question may be safely treated as anomalies which can, however, be dealt with through hypothetical adjustments of expenditure.

However, I have to qualify all the above answers with the strict condition that the value of or expenditure on an item can be weighed up and offset only against the cost of another item of the same type. For example, the current value of a durable item, say a scooter, in a household's possession can be weighed up and offset only against the estimated cost of an unmet criterion revolving around another durable item, say a mobile phone. Likewise, the excess expenditure, if any, on fulfilling a criterion involving non-durable goods, say necessities of personal hygiene, can be compared with and offset only against the cost of making up for the deficit, if any, in the fulfillment of another criterion involving non-durable goods only.

Apart from those questions, the question of diverse realities at individual and household levels must be addressed. Being a geographically massive country, India is inhabited by culturally, racially and religiously diverse groups of people with diverse socio-economic circumstances, lifestyles and dietary habits. A few examples may also be cited for the sake of a degree of specificity. To begin with, households in some urban areas enjoy free access to drinking water, yet households in many other urban areas have to buy it. Differences among individuals in terms of age, height, weight, etc. also call for different requirements, implying different expenditures. For instance, a six-foot-tall man normally means larger clothing and therefore, higher expenditure than another five-foot-tall man. Many rural households have the geographical advantage of being located in the close environs of dense forest from where they can occasionally collect tinder for use as supplementary cooking fuel and edible wild fungi, leaves and roots to supplement food requirements, whereas many other rural households do not have such advantage.

In view of such diverse realities, it makes little sense to classify the vast population of India into two categories only – rural and urban – and go on to assess whether a person/household is poor or not on the basis of the corresponding poverty lines. As the country's poverty lines make no allowance for those diverse realities of its 1.3 billion population, spread across an expansive area of 3.28 million square kilometers, India's poverty estimates cannot be accurate enough to show the actual extent of poverty in the country.

Indeed, the tradition of applying the rural and urban poverty lines to all corresponding areas may be dismissed as a methodological oversimplification of the process of identifying poor persons/households and estimating the extent of poverty in India. Why? Suppose there are two five-member households in a rural area with one consisting of a nine-year-old boy, his parents and grandparents, all aged between 30 and 55 years, and the other of a middle-age couple and their three children, all aged between 9 and 14 years. The mere difference between the two households in terms of their age composition or adult-minor ratios means that they require different minimum levels of income to fulfill the $3_{TC}+6_{NC}$ set. In other words, as adults normally need more food and toiletries and larger clothing than minors, the household with the higher adult-minor ratio needs a higher minimum level of income to fulfill the $3_{TC}+6_{NC}$ set than the other, provided that they face the same price level. It is now crystal clear that just because the two households have five members each and are located in the same category area does not mean that they need the same minimum level of income to meet the same set of criteria. To put it another way, it is arbitrary and unrealistic to apply the same poverty line to every person/household just because they live in the same category area.

For a more realistic process of deciding whether a person/household is poor or not and measuring the extent of poverty in an area or community, the poverty line should be superseded by the concept of the Socio-economic Status Scale (to be hereafter referred to as 'the S3' as a shorthand), which I have devised, keeping in mind the inherent demerits of the application of the fixed rural and urban poverty lines in a vastly diverse country like India. Apart from whatever practical can be expected of the concept of the poverty line, absolute or relative, the **S3** has, inter alia, the distinct added advantage of being able to measure the degree of poverty at all levels – individual, household, regional, national or global. Though the nine criteria that I use for determining poverty may have similarities with those of the Multidimensional Poverty Index (MPI), most of the reasons that I took into account for adopting them are apparently different from those relating to the MPI indicators. Moreover, some of the identified weaknesses of the MPI, such as its inherent inability to capture inequality and the arbitrary cut-off level, can be eliminated with the application of this concept.

Now, let me present the **S3** in its diagrammatic form for ease of analysis and assimilation, along with the table of weights in percentage terms assigned to the $3_{TC}+6_{NC}$ set per criterion.

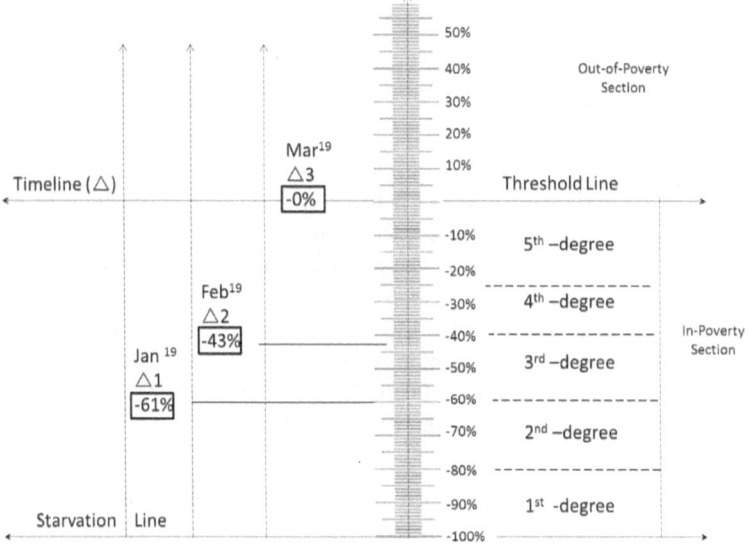

Figure 1.1 : Socio-economic Status Scale (S3)

---

Δ   Timeline doubles up as the threshold line between the Out-of-Poverty and In-Poverty/ sections.

Δ1  H's Point of Occurrence along the S3 in January 2019.

Δ2  H's Point of Occurrence along the S3 in February 2019.

Δ3  H's Point of Occurrence along the S3 in March 2019.

## Table 1.6: Weights of $3_{TC}+6_{NC}$ set

| Sl. No. | Criterion | Weight Assigned | Weight Earned (WE) |
|---|---|---|---|
| 1 | Just Adequate Food | 35% | $A \times 35/100 = WE_1$ |
| 2 | Own Dwelling | 20% | $A \times 20/100 = WE_2$ |
| 3 | Just Adequate Clothing | 12% | $A \times 12/100 = WE_3$ |
| 4 | Education | 9% | $A \times 9/100 = WE_4$ |
| 5 | Necessities of Personal Hygiene | 7% | $A \times 7/100 = WE_5$ |
| 6 | Savings/Cash in Reserve | 6% | $A \times 6/100 = WE_6$ |
| 7 | Bank Account | 4.5% | $A \times 4.5/100 = WE_7$ |
| 8 | Mobile Phone | 3.5% | $A \times 3.5/100 = WE_8$ |
| 9 | TV Set | 3% | $A \times 3/100 = WE_9$ |
| | TOTAL | 100% | $\sum_{i=1}^{n=9} WE_i$ |

NB: (i) Some money value (MV) is to be assigned to each criterion of the $3_{TC}+6_{NC}$ set. A is the percentage of the MV actually met for the corresponding criterion, whereas WE is the weight actually earned for it. For example, if 200 INR is the MV of a criterion, say necessities of personal hygiene, for a household and it manages to spend 160 INR on the criterion in question, then the actual weight earned vis-à-vis that criterion is 80×70/100=5.6%. But if the household spends 220 INR on the same criterion, which is 110% of its MV, then the actual weight earned is 110×7/100=7.7%.

(ii) No scientifically established rules were followed in the process of assigning weights to the $3_{TC}+6_{NC}$ set. Rather I had to rely on my own perceptions about the relative importance of the criteria. However, a revision of the weights will have no implications for any other aspect of the concept of the Social Status Scale than the combinations of WE's determining different degrees of poverty.

(iii) Only if the first three criteria of the $3_{TC}+6_{NC}$ set, i.e. $3_{TC}$ – so-called *Roti, Kapda Aur Makaan* – are fully met, will the A's become operational. This is an essential condition for the elimination of the potential problem of the sum of WE's falsely showing a poor

As we can make out, the vertical axis of the diagram represents the **S3**, which is intersected by the horizontal timeline exactly at 0, the threshold point dividing the **S3** into two sections – upper/out-of-poverty and lower /in-poverty sections. The former is a linear series of positive values and can also be broken up into two subsections corresponding to the out-of-poverty categories of households – middle-class and upper-class categories. But poverty being the primary theme of this paper, the diagram has been constructed in such a way as to highlight the in-poverty section in particular and help explain how and why the **S3** is a better alternative to the poverty line. The in-poverty section is linearly calibrated in negative percentage terms with its bottom value, 100%, representing starvation.

The in-poverty section is also subdivided into five equal subsections with the bottom subsection, i.e. the range between -81% and -100%, representing the worst/first-degree stage of poverty, wherein people cannot even afford just adequate food and the top subsection, ranging from -1% to -20%, constituting the least serious/fifth-degree stage of poverty.

As a household fulfills any one or more criteria of the $3_{TC}$+ $6_{NC}$ set, it earns the weights as calculated in the weight earned (WE) column of Table 1.6. The sum of the WE's is to be offset against -100%, the bottom value of the red/in-poverty section so as

household at an out-of-poverty level. For example, while failing to fulfill the criterion of an own dwelling, if a household manages to meet the rest of the $3_{TC}$+$6_{NC}$ set with that of just adequate food met at 140%, just adequate clothing at 170% and the others at 100 each, the sum of the household's WE's is:

=> (140×35/100)%+0%+(170×12/100)%+9%+7%+6%+4.5%+3.5%+3%

=> 49%+0%+20.4%+9%+7%+6%+4.5%+3.5%+3%

=> 102.4%

Offsetting it against -100%, we get 2.4, which is above 0 and located along the out-of-poverty section of the S3, thus falsely showing the household to be out of poverty; though in reality it is still in poverty because of its inability to own a dwelling of at least semi-*pucca* standards.

to accurately determine the household's actual point of occurrence along the S3.

Now, let me bring up the hypothetical case of a household denoted by **H**. As shown in Diagram 1.1, **H** is located at -61% (Δ1) along the in-poverty section of the S3 in January 2019, implying that in that month **H** earns a combined weight value of 39%, which gets offset against -100%. Then in February 2019, **H** is shown located at 43% (Δ2) along the in-poverty section of the **S3**, which falls in the third-degree stage of poverty. This means that in February 2019, **H** earns a combined weight value of 57%. But in March 2019, **H** gets nudged upwards to 0 (Δ3), the threshold point dividing the out-of-poverty section from the in-poverty one, implying that **H** manages to earn 100% in weights by perfectly fulfilling the $3_{TC}+ 6_{NC}$ set. So **H** is no longer a poor household in March 2019.

The hypothetical case of **H** has categorically illustrated how to assess whether a household is in or out of poverty at any point, or over a given period, of time with the aid of the **S3**, and, if in poverty, even measure its degree by means of the in-poverty section of the **S3**. Indeed, the concept of the **S3** and its adoption can overcome many problems that unavoidably arise when the fixed poverty line is employed in the process of deciding whether a person/household is poor or not and estimating the extent of poverty in an area or community. As the **S3** emphasizes the actual fulfillment of criteria rather than the attainment of a minimum level of income or spending, which is at the core of the application of the poverty line, many issues like inter-temporal and spatial price differentials and diversity in socio-economic circumstances of households are of little or no consequence if it is adopted and employed.

As a mechanism for assessing whether a person/household is in or out of poverty and measuring its degree, if in poverty, the **S3**, combined with the $3_{TC}+ 6_{NC}$ set, can be applied to a state, region or the whole country. Since the $3_{TC}+ 6_{NC}$ set represents the minimum present-day requirements that every person or household must fully meet, irrespective of socio-economic category, caste, culture, religion, or region, to be able to catch up and keep up with society in its increasingly competitive environment, its universal applicability and practicality cannot be questioned. Indeed, the combination of the S3 and $3_{TC}+ 6_{NC}$ set makes it absolutely practicable to ascertain accurately enough whether a person/household is in or out of poverty and, if in poverty, accurately measure its degree as well.

When more accurate data on poverty becomes available, the country's planning, formulation and implementation of well-targeted anti-poverty measures will become a lot easier, more efficient and, therefore, likelier to ultimately lead the country to victory in its protracted war against poverty.

## Chapter Two

# THE STRATEGY FOR ERADICATION OF POVERTY THROUGH INTENSIVE DEVELOPMENT OF HUMAN CAPITAL AND DEMOCRATIC REDISTRIBUTION OF PHYSICAL CAPITAL

> "Give a man a fish and you feed him for a day; teach a man to fish (and also kit him out) and you feed him for a lifetime."
>
> An adage of disputed origin and the bracketed section is mine.

What is the biggest challenge confronting the Republic of India in the first half of the 21$^{st}$ century, the so-called century of Asia? If you happen to think that is one of the much-publicized issues like the vexed Sino-Indian boundary dispute, Kashmir issue, so-called Left Wing Extremism, insurgency in the northeast, economic growth and growing religious extremism, then you are mistaken. But you cannot be blamed for that. Indeed, you are not to know that poverty is the biggest challenge that India faces today, because it is hardly recognized as that. Nor does it get as much attention from the State and media as the other issues do, resulting in the general population getting desensitized to the issue of poverty. What is in reality the biggest issue for the country of over 1.3

billion people continues to remain something of a non-priority on the national agenda. This is really an increasingly unsettling situation, with the absolute number of the poor populace ever rising in this country.

Let me give you a couple of reasons why poverty is actually the biggest challenge, or rather, threat to the country, at least in my view. Unlike most other issues like the Indo-Pakistan hostility over Kashmir and insurgency in the north-east, which are, in a manner of speaking, localized and whose direct repercussions are mostly confined to the affected areas or regions, poverty remains a pan-India problem and also the largest killer by far, not sparing any state or UT of the country. Though it is absolutely desirable to effectively handle every single problem, be it crime, unemployment or corruption, and successfully resolve every single dispute, be it the Sino-Indian border dispute or the Naga issue, because the nation stands to greatly benefit from their being effectively handled and successfully resolved, it is the eradication of poverty by developing and utilizing the massive untapped human capital of their country's poor population that can actually help propel the Indian economy on a high growth trajectory over the long term and transform India into a real economic powerhouse, which will, in turn, help realize the nation's collective dream of becoming a 'super' nation where chronic socio-economic problems like hunger, malnutrition, homelessness and poverty get wiped out or reduced to the minimum and which the world will ultimately recognize as a reliable and responsible superpower capable of leading the human world as per the Indian philosophy of *Vasudhaiva Kutumbakam* in changing the earth into a more peaceful, greener and prosperous planet for the present civilization and posterity to live in.

Before moving on to my plan for eradicating what I perceive to be the biggest challenge confronting India, that is, poverty, I feel compelled to highlight some relevant facts and figures vis-à-vis the socio-economic conditions of the country. Estimating as per the methodology of the Suresh Tendulkar committee, there were 354 million Indians or 29.6% of the population in poverty in 2009–10 and 269.3 million or 21.9% in 2011–12. But according to the 2014 report of another committee – so-called Rangarajan committee – the estimates of Indians living in poverty were 454 million or 38.20% of the population in 2009–10 and 363 million or 29.50% in 2011–12. The difference between the estimates of the two committees resulted from the different poverty lines set by them: 27 INR and 33 INR per day for rural and urban areas respectively, set by the Suresh Tendulkar committee; and 32 INR and 47 INR per day for rural and urban areas respectively, set by the Rangarajan committee.

The disagreement between the poverty estimates of the two expert committees puts a big question mark against their reliability, notwithstanding the fact that both show a downward trend in the extent of poverty. Though poverty can be seen to have fallen from the 1951–55 average of 52.66% to 21.90 % of the total population in 2011–12 (based on Tendulkar methodology) or 29.5% in 2011–12 (Rangarajan committee estimate), the number of Indians living in poverty has actually risen from 198.7 million in 1951–55 to 269.3 million (Tendulkar committee estimate) or 363 million (Rangarajan committee estimate) in 2011–12. These opposite trends in percentage and absolute terms speak volumes for the failure of India's anti-poverty measures.

According to the 2011 census, there were 1.77 million homeless people in India, who live on railway platforms, roadsides, etc. To provide them with proper shelter, we need a budgetary allocation of about 12,000 crore INR, which is less than the estimated amount of loans systematically defaulted by Nirav Modi and the estimated value (roughly 2 billion USD) of Antilia, the home of the country's richest man, Mr. Mukesh Ambani, which was ironically built on a plot of land originally meant for an orphanage. Such facts throw into question the conscience of the powers that be as well as the legitimacy of the system running the country!

In July 2015, Mr. Arun Jaitley, then finance minister, released the findings of the Socio Economic and Caste Census (SECC) 2011, which brought to the fore many important facts and figures about the miserable conditions under which millions of Indians languish. According to the SECC 2011, there are as many as 23.70 million landless families living in houses of one room with '*kachcha*' (impermanent) walls and roof and 53.70 millions landless households earning the best part of their income from manual labour. Though the Census 2011 recorded that 32% of the rural population were illiterate, the SECC 2011 revised the figure upwards at 36% or 319 million rural persons. Even among the 64% literate rural population, more than one fifth have not completed high school. For most of them, life remains a constant struggle for survival without any real prospects for them to be able to grow socio-economically on their own.

When I first saw the mention of families living in one-room houses with '*kachcha*' walls and roof in the SECC 2011 report, what suddenly ran through my mind were my own childhood memories of living in one such house. Indeed, I can still remember the 'earthly' smell of the mud walls of my family's one-room dwelling, under the edges of whose thatch sparrows built their nests. With a bit of nostalgia, I do still remember watching the 'smoky' struggle of my mother or one of my sisters to keep the firewood burning by blowing through a bamboo pipe as she cooked food in one corner of the single-room house, getting those distracting itchy mosquito bites while doing my school homework by the light of a kerosene lamp, sitting and kneeling on a jute bag laid on the cold mud floor, playfully feeling the small depressions on the mud floor left by the drips of rainwater penetrating though the thinning spots of the thatch and moving from my father's plate to my mother's just to eat a little more food during the supper were some of my daily childhood experiences. One particularly special memory is that of my mother cutting a square piece of cloth from her disused pink '*innaphi*' (a rectangular piece of cloth traditionally worn around their torso by married Manipuri women) for me to use as a handkerchief at school.

If I may digress a little further and add some more poverty-related experiences of my childhood, I do have some funny but unforgettable school memories.♤ My beloved mother was a local fish vendor, who was known in our locality for her hard-working nature, honesty and humility; and my father was a politically well-connected and well-known figure,€ who could also be aptly termed a 'local statesman of principled but impractical politics.' Despite being in poverty, they somehow managed to ensure my schooling from English-medium schools. As my father used to be late for my monthly school fees, being chased up by the school administration for payment of overdue fees, especially in the run-up to examinations, was a frequent experience of my schooldays. I was also at the receiving end of taunts from some of my classmates actually from my very first day at St. Mary's High School, my first

---

♤ Bringing up such school memories should not be wrongly interpreted as trying to tarnish the image of St. Mary's High School, which I always hold in high esteem; and I will not hesitate to even admit that it was on the basis of my primary education there that I have managed to build up whatever academic capacity is there in me today. Nor should it be construed as expressing any kind of ill feeling against any of my former classmates, the childish bullies included; and I have a lot of love and respect for all of them. Indeed, the only intention in bringing them up is to highlight the fact that the socio-psychological impact of poverty is also felt even among school students.

€ One may wonder how a politically well-connected and well-known figure's family would be in poverty. But that is the truth about my family. Despite being a senior member of the Manipur Pradesh Congress Committee and President of the party's Lamsang Kendra Committee, my beloved father literally spent all his life in poverty. Indeed, at many major political functions, my old father, always in *Khadi dhoti* and *kurta,* used to share dais with ministers, MP's and MLA's, including former chief ministers of Manipur late Messrs Rishang Keishing and W. Nipamacha Singh, deputy chief minister Dr. L. Chandramani Singh and MP Mr. Thounoujam Chaoba Singh. At most of those political functions, I saw and heard the good orator in my beloved father delivering

English-medium school. I did not know that a teacher was to be addressed as Sir or Miss/Madam at the school. So I yelled, 'Oja' – meaning teacher in Manipuri – at the class teacher as I wanted to complain against one of my new classmates for pulling my hair from behind; and on hearing that loud yell, the whole class instantly burst into laughter. The class teacher, Miss Kimboi, somehow silenced the class immediately, apparently amused herself though. From that day onwards, some 'unruly' classmates often made fun of me by shouting 'Oja' at me. Later on I came to be taunted for many other reasons also, such as living in a thatched house, in front of which I used to stand waiting for the school jeep, wearing a pair of stinking rubber shoes, carrying plain rice and *sabji* as tiffin and so on. Actually, the taunts made me feel as though I was somewhat different from them; a kind of inferiority feeling it was. Though those happenings and taunts seem childish and funny in retrospection, they made my school days very miserable indeed. I also remember taking recourse to even

---

political speeches and also drawing applause. I also remember *laal-bati* cars stopping by our one-room thatched house on a few occasions. But perhaps the principal occupants of those cars were least interested in the conditions under which their *'ahan-ibungo'* – a respectful way of addressing a party veteran in Manipuri – was living. That some people used to visit my father to discuss the allotment of party tickets during elections also speaks volumes for the level of stock that he once enjoyed in the state committee of the 'Grand Old Party.' Though a practising Gandhian, he never hesitated to risk his own life by daring to hoist the *charkha* tri-colour every morning in the front of our thatched house and remaining actively involved in the activities of the party even during the peak period of insurgency in Manipur. It is no exaggeration to say that the Indian National Congress grew up in Manipur on the shoulders of the likes of my father. But he died a poor man that he had been throughout his life, in his humble abode with mud and straw walls, thanks to his Gandhian outlook and principled but impractical politics, when politics in India then was, today is, and will most likely remain, only a power-seeking process primarily involving confusing and fooling the masses in the most 'trustworthy' fashion, along with the constant deployment of sophisticated political propaganda, especially 'nice, high-sounding and comforting' political doublespeak, exaggerations, lies and sophistries.

falsehood so as to silence those irritating taunts at school. I once boosted to some classmates, though falsely, that the mud and straw walls of my house were layered with brick walls from inside for two special purposes: first to protect my family from stray bullets in case of a shootout between security forces and militants, which was quite a frequent occurrence in Manipur then; and second to avoid getting served with donation-seeking notes from militant groups as there was a trend of these groups demanding money from people living in brick houses, which were once identified with affluence in Manipur. And, amusingly enough, my classmates took that for granted, though I could see a common expression of surprise and even childish envy in the face of most of them, especially the annoying big bullies. Indeed, that was how I managed to get some irritating classmates to stop taunting me about my thatched house, which also had blue polythene sheets spread over its roof as a Band-Aid for leaks, treat me with some respect and also allow me to join them at play sometimes.

On a more serious note, being someone who almost never got to eat food to his heart's content during his entire childhood, except on special occasions, of course, and has also gone through a range of other poverty-related experiences first-hand, it is quite easy and natural for me to empathize with those poor households living in dwellings of one room each with *kuchcha* walls and roof, owning no agricultural land and surviving on income from manual casual labour. Notwithstanding the enormous food subsidy annually budgeted in the name of the poor, it has always been an uphill struggle for these poor households to afford adequate food. This is not surprising in view of the fact that the SECC 2011 registered a whopping 13,39,85,215 Indian households whose highest earners earn less than 5,000 INR a month. The miserable conditions under which these households survive are like a prison from which they virtually have no practical means to break free. Indeed, they remain an unwilling burden on the country's finances with the government spending thousands of crores of rupees on numerous socio-economic welfare programmes purportedly meant to enable the poor to come out of poverty. But India's anti-poverty schemes do not go any beyond preventing extreme hunger and starvation and ensuring the 'minimal' survival of the poor, with their funds getting siphoned off at multiple points.

Renowned economists Arvind Panagariya and Jagdish Bhagwati claim in an article[1] that taking account of corruption and leakages, the NREGA essentially spends as much as 248 INR in order to deliver a net 50 INR per person per day. This means that the government spends 4.96 INR to deliver one rupee's worth of benefits to the poor. According to another write-up[2], out of every rupee spent on the food subsidy scheme, only 12 paise reaches the right beneficiary.

A press release by the World Bank on 18 May 2011, "India's Poor Yet to Reap Full Benefits of Its Anti-Poverty Programmes",[3] on its report, "Social Protection for a Changing India", states that according to the 2004–05 NSS, only 41% of the grains released by the government reach households, with some states doing much worse and the Planning Commission putting the figure of the leakage of BPL grains at 58% nationally in 2001. It further states that the MGNREGA does not guarantee 100 days of work per rural household just yet and unfulfilled demand for work is high even when 25% MGNREGA funds were not spent with fund utilization rate ranging from 56% in Tamil Nadu to 89% in Rajasthan. These figures also bring to the fore the fact that the social protection and poverty alleviation programmes of India are actually riddled with inefficiencies and unarguably prone to massive leakages and corruption at multiple level. Indeed, they have more the effect of lining the pockets of corrupt politicians, officials and agents than of tiding the poor population over.

---

1. *http://blogs.timesofindia.indiatimes.com/toi-edit-page/rural-inefficiencyactdespiteprotestsabout-diluting-nrega-the-pm-is-right-to-confine-it-to-200-poorest-districts/*

2. *http://firstbiz.firstpost.com/economy/right-food-right-loot-rs-1-lakh-crore-foodsubsidywillreachpoor-77822.html*

3. *http://web.worldbank.org/WBSITE/EXTERNAL/NEWS/0,,pagePK:34382~pIPK:34439~theSitePK:4607,00.HTML*

It is true that India is a highly populous country with over 1.3 billion people today. So the gigantic size of its population has to be a major factor in its prolonged failure to efficiently implement its numerous big-ticket anti-poverty programmes and social security and welfare schemes. However, glancing through the poverty-related statistics of China, the world's most populous country, it can be seen that China has successfully pulled off a number of its anti-poverty programmes, thus helping millions of its poor people come out of poverty. According to the World Development Indicators data released by the World Bank, China has managed to bring the number of its poor population from 884 million in 1981 down to 25 million only in 2003, estimated on the basis of the World Bank's poverty line of 1.9 USD per day. Referring to the poverty data of the National Bureau of Statistics of China, it is found that the number of poor people in China fell from 250 million in 1978 to 15 million 2007 with an annual reduction rate of 9.2% when measured with its 1978 poverty line. But in India the number of people in poverty fell from 329 million in 1977–78 (Indian Economic Survey 2001–02) to 269.3 million in 2011–12 (estimate based on Tendulkar methodology). So it may be concluded that there has been a very wide 'success' gap between the anti-poverty programmes of India, the world's largest democracy, and those of China, a one-party regime, which has come to be described by Western scholars as a state capitalist system. Though the significantly different economic growth trajectories of the two most populous countries may explain the wide success gap between their anti-poverty measures to some extent, China has been by far more successful in reducing poverty than India primarily because of the following broadly discussed different realities of the two countries:

i. China invests a great deal of its resources in its systematic holistic development of the human capital of its poor people, whereas India's programmes for the poor show a clear lack of trust in the socio-economic potential of its poor population and so do not go much beyond ensuring their minimal survival.

ii. China has seamlessly integrated its anti-poverty policy into the national development strategy, whereas India does not follow a proactive path to poverty alleviation and its anti-poverty programmes lack coordination at all levels.

iii. China is able to concentrate its available private and public resources on deserving households, villages, counties and regions. But electoral considerations in India prevent the folks in power from initiating well-targeted anti-poverty measures and its available resources, therefore, get thinly dispersed in a please-all manner.

iv. In China, policy/programme course correction is a swift process, whereas in India it is like a labyrinthine nightmare.

v. The level of corruption is significantly lower in China than India, because the former enforces a strict code of conduct on its party and administrative officials. Also, China's anti-corruption law provides for the death penalty and its system of justice is comparatively efficient and swift, whereas it takes years and even decades – remember the fodder scam cases – for the Indian judiciary to dispose of corruption cases, thus giving the corrupt a very good chance of serving their sentence in their own graves.

Indeed, the different systems of government offer different environment of governance in India and China. Though India, being a democratic polity, performs better than China on some human development indicators – human rights, press freedom, political liberty, etc. – and can also claim the moral high ground, it cannot be denied that China has outperformed India in a number of other areas like science and technology, housing for its people, drinking water availability, employment and, more importantly, education. So it makes sense for India to take a leaf out of China's book in terms of developing the human capital of the poor and tackling poverty effectively. If you ask a poor but rational man to make choice between the right to vote and getting adequate food to eat, he will not take a split second to choose the latter, though it may be argued that both choices are not mutually exclusive in a democratic country like India.

In an article entitled, "Countering Growing Inequality",[4] Pulapre Balakrishnan (Professor of Ashoka University and Senior Fellow of IIM, Kozhikode) compares the income share of the top 1% of the Indian population with that of China. Citing the *World Inequality Report 2018*, he writes in the article that the income share of the top 1% of the Chinese population is 14%, whereas the corresponding figure of India is 22%, which is even higher than the British Raj's record share of the top 1% in national income, which stood at 20.7% in 1939–40. Since 1980, the Indian economy has grown 200%, whereas it is 800% for China. But the level of income inequality in China is by far less than India's. The rising income inequality in India also reinforces the theory that the growth pattern of the Indian economy has been biased towards the upper income group.

Citing Ahya and Sheth, P Topalova writes in, "Is the Rising Tide Lifting All Boats?",[5] that the increase in wealth in India between 2003 and 2007 was equal to the country's GDP in 2007, with the equity market, residential property market and gold being the three key sources of wealth. Ahya and Sheth are further cited as concluding that wealth accretion in India has been concentrated in a very small segment of the population with only 4% to 7% of the population participating in the stock market, less than half, or about 47%, owning a *pucca* dwelling and the top 35% of Indian households owning 71% of the value of consumer durables, including gold and valuable jewellery.

---

4. *http://www.thehindu.com/opinion/lead/countering-growing-inequality/article22282400.ece*
5. P. Topalova (2008): "*Is the Rising Tide Lifting All Boats?*" IMF Working Papers 08/54

Citing a 2010 study, P. Lanjouw, R. Murgai, et al., write in, "*Rising Inequality: A Cause for Concern?*",[6] that between 1996 and 2008, wealth holdings of Indian billionaires rose from 0.8% of the GDP to 23%. In 2004–05, the level of consumption inequality in India as measured by the Gini Coefficient rose to 0.51 in 2013. According to the Credit Suisse's *Global Wealth Databook* for 2014, the bottom 10% of the Indian population owned merely 0.2% of the national wealth, whereas the top 10% owned a whopping 74%. The wealth share of the richest 10% of Indians further swelled to 80.70% in 2016. The *World Inequality Report* 2018, which was published by the World Inequality Lab and is part of the *World Wealth and Income Database* project, shows that the income share of the top 10% of Indians was 55% in 2016, whereas the corresponding figures of China and the European Union were 41% and 34% respectively.

Between 1992 and 2014, the income share of the richest 10% of the Indian population grew from 34% to 54.20 %, which is nearly four times the income share of the bottom 50% of Indians, estimated at 15.30%.

All the above income- and wealth-related statistics of India are undeniable evidence of the fact that a grossly disproportionate amount of income and, therefore, wealth has accrued to the richest from the country's economic growth, especially in the wake of the introduction of the economic reform trinity – liberalization, privatization and globalization – in the early 1990s. But the critical question is, how can India arrest the continuous accumulation of the benefits of economic growth by the superrich, who control the country's capital? Indeed, there are many radical policy changes, for example, raising the income tax rates for the two top slabs and bringing in a universal basic income scheme, which can be

---

6. Peter Lanjouw, Rinku Murgai, et al., "*Rising Inequality: A Cause for Concern?*" Perspective on Poverty in India, World Bank.

\# The Gini Coefficient is a statistical measure of inequality, with a value of 0 denoting complete equality and 1 maximum inequality.

made so as to bring about a speedy reversal of the outrageously disproportionate concentration of wealth and capital in the hands of the superrich. But it is hardly possible for an increasingly capitalist democracy like India to go the revolutionary way in bringing about a socio-economic paradigm shift.

So India must develop and pursue an organically redistributive economic development model with a human face and also some amount of humanitarian prejudice in favour of the poor so that the country can put itself on a truly inclusive and balanced growth path. It is on the strength of my belief in such a national imperative that I have formulated the **Strategy for Eradication of Poverty through Intensive Development of Human Capital and Democratic Redistribution of Physical Capital,** to be hereafter referred to as the SEP(IDHC&DRPC), which can, I am confident, help transform the poor from a massive burden on the country's exchequer into another growth locomotive of the Indian economy and eradicate poverty in the process.

## PRESENTING THE SEP(IDHC&DRPC)

Even after seven decades of independence, millions of Indian households, including my own, still continue to languish in poverty mainly because of the incompetence of the country's successive governments, which have always sold the poor down the river after coming to power primarily by means of their votes. Indeed, there is one underlying reason why India has miserably failed to eradicate poverty even after witnessing high economic growth in the last three decades. For the country's political elite, the poor are nothing more than an enormous mass of *karmic* burden that has to be carried through by means of subsides and limited employment guarantee schemes for all eternity. Their condemnable inability to properly appreciate the huge economic potential of the poor is what prevents them and the bureaucracy from thinking and going beyond unskilled employment programmes for the poor and general subsidies, which apparently have only cosmetic effect on the challenging phenomenon of poverty. In consequence, the human capital of the poor, which must be the focus of attention for dealing with poverty, remains neglected and does not find enough importance in the so-called poverty alleviation policy and programmes of the country. Interestingly enough, there are also some schemes that have been packaged as "investment in capacity building" for the poor. But the only capacity built, if at all, via such schemes cannot be anything more than the one to endure poverty without much complaining. Is that what the poor are actually entitled to, by virtue of their birth in and citizenship of the world's largest democracy and third largest economy in purchasing-power-parity terms?

No, the poor are actually entitled to a lot more than what the democratic State has given them thus far. Indeed, they are naturally entitled to the overall means to adequately realize their potential and stand on their own feet. In other words, they all deserve to be weaned off the protracted undignified subsidized living once and for all. So how can the poor be given what they actually deserve?

The SEP(IDHC&DRPC) offers a direct answer.

But before I go on to elaborate on the SEP(IDHC&DRPC), let me write a little about something that is quite conspicuous by its absence. It is a matter of amazement and concern that India has yet to establish a dedicated ministry to deal with the poor, though the country has ministries of Tribal Affairs, Railways, Steel, Textiles, etc. This fact stinks of a very casual and cavalier attitude of the State towards the poor as well as the chronic issue of poverty. The prolonged absence of what may be called 'Anti-Poverty Ministry' is a big or maybe the biggest reason why India has miserably failed to surmount poverty, which continues to affect no less than 200 million Indians, which is only a conservative official estimate.

As the country's poverty alleviation programmes are not under the supervision of a single dedicated ministry, there is always a serious lack of coordination among the existing anti-poverty programmes, resulting in a skewed distribution of benefits. This does not, however, mean that a better coordination among all the anti-poverty programmes will make up for all the deficiencies in the country's overall approach to poverty. So it is imperative that India establishes a dedicated ministry to deal effectively with poverty by bringing all anti-poverty programmes under its direct control and supervision. Such a strategic step will certainly prove to be a giant leap in the right direction in the country's uphill struggle against poverty, let there be no doubt.

Now coming back to the SEP(IDHC&DRPC), it will not be practical for this strategy to cover the entire poor population in one go. So the only option is to implement it in a phased manner, albeit on a military footing, with the selection of beneficiaries to be carried out on the basis of the poorest-first principle for the obvious reason that it is the poorest of the poor who survive under the worst of conditions and, therefore, deserve priority treatment. Indeed, the SEP(IDHC&DRPC) may be basically broken down into two parts --- IDHC and DRPC --- which are successively elaborated below.

## PART I: INTENSIVE DEVELOPMENT OF HUMAN CAPITAL(IDHC)

One of the prime reasons why millions of households remain helplessly trapped in poverty is the inadequacy of their human capital. This implies that for any anti-poverty drive to be effective, it has to focus on human capital of the poor too. The IDHC part of the SEP(IDHC&DRPC) focuses upon human capital of the poor and is basically formed of the following steps:

### *Step 1– Comprehensive Survey of Poor Households*

A comprehensive survey of all poor households must be conducted so as to create a 360-degree profile of every poor household, accurately detailing the following aspects:

## 1.1 Size and General Composition of A Poor Household

Data on the size and general composition of a poor household will play a critical role in determining what line of trade its eligible members may be chosen for. For example, if a poor household consists of two adults, say a husband and wife , and their two children both aged under 10 years, both the adults are not supposed to be trained in trades requiring long stays away from home, implying that one or both of them must be trained in some home-based trade so that at least one remains at home to take care of their two children too. On the other hand, for an all-adult poor household, it may not matter much whether its members are trained in home-based trades or others involving staying/working away from home.

## 1.2 Status/Nature of Dwelling

Detailed information on the status/nature of a poor household's dwelling is important in the process of making a customized plan to empower/enable it to come out of poverty.

## 1.3 Physical and Socio-Economic Geography of Household Location

Detailed information on the physical and socio-economic geography of a poor household's location is essential for the construction of a proper customized plan to bring it out of poverty. For example, if there is an acute shortage of pork supply in a particular region, say the north-east, it makes sense to train some poor households in this region in pig farming and provide them with the required capital to start a pig farm as part of the customized plans to bring them out of poverty. For other poor households located in parts of the jute belt in West Bengal, their eligible members ought to be trained in making jute items and provided with the required physical capital to establish cottage factories for manufacturing jute items.

## 1.4 Personal Profiles of Household Members

A comprehensive personal profile of every member of a poor household must be created within its 360-degree profile with the following details as key elements:

1.4.1 Personal details such as sex, age and height are crucial for determining what kind of trade will suit an eligible poor person better. For example, a male will better make a pickup driver than a female; and, a 25-year-old man is more suitable to be trained as an excavator operator than a 45-year-old man.

1.4.2 The IQ level of every eligible person must be assessed and reflected in their respective personal profiles.

1.4.3 Information on the health of every eligible person must also be included in his or her personal profile so that medical intervention/treatment can be provided, if needed. Indeed, keeping the poor healthy and strong is itself an essential part of the process of enabling them to come out of poverty.

1.4.4 Information on previous work experience/skills, if any, is also important for the process of selecting specific trades for eligible poor persons. So such information must be given a prominent position in the personal profile of every eligible poor person

## Step 2 – Selection of Poor Households for Successive Coverage under the SEP(IDHC&DRPC)

Given the enormous size of the poor population in India, it will not be practical for the SEP(IDHC&DRPC) to cover all the poor households in one go. So it will have to cover them in batches with the poorest of the poor to be selected first on the basis of the poorest-first principle. However, a poor household being covered by the SEP(IDHC&DRPC) does not mean that all its eligible members will be trained and provided with physical capital.

Indeed, how many eligible members of a poor household are chosen for direct action under the SEP(IDHC&DRPC) will be determined on the basis of its strength or size. If, for example, a poor household consists of five members, of whom two are eligible for direct action, one of the two can be chosen as direct beneficiary and the rest automatically become indirect beneficiaries. This implies that if one crore poor persons are chosen as direct beneficiaries, there will also be four crore indirect beneficiaries under the SEP(IDHC&DRPC).

However, as household strengths do not vary only by the multiples of five, the problem of household strength variation has to be dealt with through a mechanism for choosing a direct beneficiary for a particular type of trade, one that not only allows for dependency ratio, but also takes into account the varying potential income levels of specific trades per unit of expenditure on training and capital allocation. For example, if two poor households have the same strength but different dependency ratios, the direct beneficiary or beneficiaries of the one with the higher dependency ratio must be chosen for a trade with a higher potential level of income.

## Step 3 – Drawing up Tailor-Made Plan of Action under the SEP(IDHC&DRPC) for Every Poor Household

Every poor household must be covered through a tailor-made plan of action to be drawn up strictly on the basis of the answers to the following questions, which are to be found in its 360-degree profile.

3.1 What are the reasons why a particular household is in poverty?

3.2 What are the current living conditions of the poor household?

3.3 What is its dependency ratio?

3.4 How many members are eligible for direct action under the SEP(IDHC&DRPC)?

3.5 What trades are relatively suitable for its eligible members?

3.6 What are the current basic requirements of the poor household as a whole?

Though the actual process of intensively developing the human capital of the poor persons chosen as direct beneficiaries is to begin only in the wake of formulation of plans of action for them, all the prerequisites like profiling of poor households and selection of their members for direct action have been incorporated into the IDHC part for the sake of structural compression of the SEP(IDHC&DRPC).

## Step 4 – Intensive Vocational and General Education Programme (IVGEP)

This step marks the beginning of the actual IDHC part, taking the form of the IVGEP. It consists of two sections: vocational and general education. Though its general education section can have a single format, the vocational education section has to be arranged in as many formats as the number of different trades to be covered by it. This is clearly because different trades mean different vocational skills, which have to be imparted via different training arrangements. For example, training in driving mostly involves outdoor activity and can normally be completed in a matter of three months, including imparting some basic insight into a motor vehicle's critical parts; whereas training in garment-making cannot have the same training format as driving. Let me present the basic formats of both the sections of the IVGEP:

### 4.1 Format of General Education

The purpose of the general education section is to impart basic literacy and numeracy skills and elementary socio-economic knowledge to those direct beneficiaries who do not possess them already, to be determined through a test in the process of creating their personal profiles. Let us have a look at its modular structure:

### Module One (First 15 Session Days)

| Sl. No. | Item | Duration Per Session Day |
|---|---|---|
| 1. | Importance of Literacy & Numeracy (Talk) | 30 Mins |
| 2. | Literacy Skills (LS) | 90 Mins |
| 3. | Numeracy Skills (NS) | 30 Mins |

### Module Two (First 15 Session Days)

| Sl. No. | Item | Duration Per Session Day |
|---|---|---|
| 1. | LS | 60 Mins |
| 2. | NS | 30 Mins |
| 3. | Hygiene & Healthy Living (Talk) | 30 Mins |

### Module Three (First 15 Session Days)

| Sl. No. | Item | Duration Per Session Day |
|---|---|---|
| 1. | LS | 60 Mins |
| 2. | NS | 30 Mins |
| 3. | Rights, Responsibilities & Socio-economic Welfare Programmes | 30 Mins |

### Module Four (First 15 Session Days)

| Sl. No. | Item | Duration Per Session Day |
|---|---|---|
| 1. | LS | 60 Mins |
| 2. | NS | 30 Mins |
| 3. | Importance & Basic Applications of Mobile Phone[+] | 30 Mins |

### Module Five (First 15 Session Days)

| Sl. No. | Item | Duration Per Session Day |
|---|---|---|
| 1. | LS | 60 Mins |
| 2. | NS | 30 Mins |
| 3. | Elementary Banking & Finance++ | 30 Mins |

### Module Six (First 15 Session Days)

| Sl. No. | Item | Duration Per Session Day |
|---|---|---|
| 1. | LS | 60 Mins |
| 2. | NS | 30 Mins |
| 3. | Basic Entrepreneurial Skills | 30 Mins |

### Module Seven (First 10 Session Days)

| Sl. No. | Item | Duration Per Session Day |
|---|---|---|
| 1. | LS | 60 Mins |
| 2. | NS | 30 Mins |
| 3. | Revision of All Other Items | 30 Mins |

So we have seen that the general education section of the IVGEP has a format consisting of seven modules with 15 session days each, except the last module, which has 10 session days for aided revision. Indeed, this section has been developed by taking into account the six basic assumptions of Malcolm Knowles' theory of Andragogy, defined as 'the art and science of helping adults learn.'

---

+ All direct beneficiaries must be provided with an entry-level mobile phone each at the beginning of Module Four.

++ During Module Five, those direct beneficiaries having no bank accounts already must be introduced into the formal financial system by opening a bank account for each of them.

We have also seen that apart from basic literacy and numeracy skills, the general education section covers some other topics which are of great importance in the socio-economic life of a person. Ensuring that direct beneficiaries acquire a workable level of knowledge on those topics plus basic literacy and numeracy skills is one of the most important elements in the development of their human capital.

## 4.2 Format of Vocational Education

As stated earlier, the vocational education section of the IVGEP will have several formats, because the format of one trade cannot be the same as that of another; and it must cover a wide range of trades like furniture-making, baking, making of leather items, ceramics and even dairy farming, which offer good business prospects and persons with an average IQ level can easily be trained in. But it is the textile sector that holds a relatively great deal of potential in terms of export and domestic market, not to mention its labour-intensive nature and dependence on agriculture, the biggest source of employment for the poor, for raw inputs. Let me, therefore, present the modular structure of vocational training in garment-making, a major segment of the textile sector, for the purposes of illustration.

### Module One (First 25 Session Days)

| Sl. No. | Item | Duration Per Session Day |
|---|---|---|
| 1. | Understanding Fabrics, Designs & Patterns | 30 Mins |
| 2. | Understanding the Machinery (Basic) | 30 Mins |
| 3. | Marking & Cutting of Cloth (Basic) | 30 Mins |
| 4. | Sewing (Basic) | 90 Mins |

### Module Two (Second 25 Session Days)

| Sl. No. | Item | Duration Per Session Day |
|---|---|---|
| 1. | Understanding the Machinery (Advanced) | 30 Mins |
| 2. | Marking & Cutting of Cloth (Advanced) | 30 Mins |
| 3. | Sewing (Advanced) | 90 Mins |
| 4. | Miscellaneous Subsidiary Skills | 30 Mins |

### Module Three (Third 25 Session Days)

| Sl. No. | Item | Duration Per Session Day |
|---|---|---|
| 1. | Machinery Repair (Minor) | 30 Mins |
| 2. | Marking & Cutting of Cloth (Specialized) | 30 Mins |
| 3. | Sewing (Specialized) | 90 Mins |
| 4. | Miscellaneous Subsidiary Skills | 30 Mins |

### Module Four (Fourth 25 Session Days)

| Sl. No. | Item | Duration Per Session Day |
|---|---|---|
| 1. | Understanding the Market (Theoretical) | 30 Mins |
| 2. | Marking & Cutting of Cloth (Real) | 30 Mins |
| 3. | Sewing (Real) | 90 Mins |
| 4. | Miscellaneous Subsidiary Skills | 30 Mins |

So the format of the vocational education section of the IVGEP vis-à-vis garment-making is composed of four modules, all of which have 25 session days and four items each. Altogether it runs into 100 session days, the same as the general education section.

The two segments of the IVGEP must be run together and a total of 5 hours and 30 minutes is its stipulated duration per session day, allowing for a 30-minute mid-session break.

By the end of the IVGEP, which can be completed in 4 months if there are 25 session days per month, every direct beneficiary can reasonably be expected to acquire not only the required skill set of a particular trade but also basic literacy and numeracy skills and some workable level of knowledge about several critical areas of life such as hygiene, personal and social values, welfare programmes, banking and use of the mobile phone, all of which will stand them and, by extension, their households in good stead in the rest of their life.

During the entire period of the IVGEP, every direct beneficiary must also be given a regular allowance to sustain themselves and their dependents.

The IVGEP must be run through its designated centres, each of which must enrol people from within a radius of 20 km, a distance that can be normally covered by public transport in a matter of an hour, implying that an IVGEP centre can cater for a catchment area of 1256.64 sq. km. For far-flung areas, the radius can be reduced to 5 km, which can be normally covered on foot in less than an hour. However, an IVGEP's size and the range of trades that it can provide training in will vary according to the density of poor households and eligible persons in the catchment area.

## PART II: DEMOCRATIC REDISTRIBUTION OF PHYSICAL CAPITAL (DRPC)

It is beyond any doubt that capital is increasingly concentrated in the hands of whom Karl Marx used to call money-bags, who control the entire production chain in today's globalised economic set-up. This is, of course, the single biggest factor in the global phenomenon of rising income inequality, as categorically presented by Thomas Piketty in his monumental work, *Capital in the Twenty-first Century*, in the form of the formula, $r>g$, with $r$ representing the average annual rate of return on capital and *g* the annual economic growth rate. In the case of India, the bottom 50% of its population had an income share of merely 15.30%, whereas the top 1% had a mindboggling 21.70% as its income share in 2014, according to the *World Inequality Report 2018*. So the question is, how can this problem of rising income inequality be arrested and also reversed? The answer obviously is redistribution of capital in favour of the poor and the underprivileged, which is the core purpose of this part of the SEP(IDHC &DRPC). Indeed, it is proposed to be implemented in the following steps:

## Step 1 – Systematic Allocation of Matching Capital to Direct Beneficiaries.

On completion of the IVGEP, all direct beneficiaries must be provided with matching capital in a systematic manner and initiated into the real world of production, thus actually enabling them to embark on an economically productive journey, which will ultimately lead them to an economically and socially prosperous life. Being systematic in the allocation of capital means that all capital requirements of every direct beneficiary are provided as per the tailor-made plans for them.

Indeed, just because a group of direct beneficiaries have been trained in a particular trade, say apparel-making, does not mean that they will all have the same capital requirements. For example, some of them may already have enough space in their respective homes to install a sewing machine, whereas some others may not have enough space in their homes to house it. In the latter case, the construction of a proper room for the sewing machine must be incorporated into the tailor-made plans for them. However, for those having no land for construction of such a room, a cluster of them can be built on a vacant piece of government-owned land that is normally reachable in a matter of an hour or so.

## Step 2 – Establishment of Information Exchange and Support System

In the initial days of production, every direct beneficiary is bound to encounter many teething troubles, particularly in the areas of networking and marketing. Such initial start-up problems have to be addressed by creating a mechanism for providing them with adequate support, especially in the form of some handholding. Further, the implementing agency must systematically monitor and keep track of their performance up to a certain stage so as to assess the SEP(IDHC & DRPC)'s overall impact and recommend changes to it, if required, for the sake of better results. So a proper information exchange and support system has to be built into the SEP(IDHC&DRPC).

By the end of the IVGEP, all direct beneficiaries are supposed to acquire the skill to operate the mobile phone at least in basic terms, which can serve as an efficient medium of information exchange. So a call centre can be set up so that every direct beneficiary can dial the implementing agency for any kind of relevant information and support that they may come to need. A direct beneficiary who has started producing something, say apparel, may initially find it somewhat difficult to understand how and where to sell/export his product for the best price. Another trained in and provided overall capital for pig farming may want to know from whom and where to get the right medicine for a disease affecting his pigs. So it may be concluded that the information exchange and support system will ensure that they enjoy a 24X7 access to the right kind of information and support.

On the other hand, the implementing agency can also call up a random sample of direct beneficiaries to collect relevant data via the information exchange and support system so as to proactively respond to the needs of direct beneficiaries. Moreover, as briefly stated above, the SEP(IDHC&DRPC) must be reviewed and reformed from time to time; and for this purpose a lot of data has to be collected from direct beneficiaries, which can be done through the information exchange and support system.

## Step 3 – Systematic Recovery of Expenditure

Given the massive size of people in poverty, it is quite clear that even a phased coverage of the poor by the SEP(IDHC&DRPC) will demand a massive annual budgetary allocation over several years. However, unlike the humongous unrecoverable bill that the Sate foots on account of food and fuel subsidies for all, there will be enough room for the State to systematically recover the expenditure on the SEP(IDHC&DRPC).

Once direct beneficiaries get into real production mode, it is certain for them to start receiving a steady flow of income. If and when their income crosses a minimum level, to be determined on a case-by-case basis with the aid of an algorithm determining how much money is required for them and their absolute dependants to maintain minimum basic standards of living, they may be made by contract and/or an incentive policy to regularly pay part of what is in excess of their minimum income level back to the exchequer as repayment of the expenditure on account of their training and provision of capital and allowances. For example, if a direct beneficiary needs 10,000 INR to meet the minimum basic standards of living and earns a net income of 15,000 INR in a certain month, he may then be required to pay some of the excess amount of 5,000 INR, say 30% to 40%, back to the exchequer for that month as an excess-income-based monthly instalment on the IDHC&DRPC expenditure on his account, with the repayment process to continue until it is fully repaid in real terms. But one valid question may be raised here: What if the direct beneficiary's net income falls short of even the minimum income level in the following month? In that case he may well be allowed to withdraw from his repaid amount the amount of money that his current net income falls short of the minimum income level, provided, of course, that the total repaid amount is equal to or more than the net income shortfall.

So basically the SEP(IDHC&DRPC) consists of two parts with one having to be implemented in four steps and the other in three steps, as shown above. However, this is not necessarily a definitive structure of the SEP(IDHC& DRPC). Indeed, there is still scope for it to be developed further.

## SOME IMPORTANT CONSIDERATIONS

Apart from the need to raise, organize and deploy a humongous army of technical and non-technical personnel, the adoption and implementation of the SEP(IDHC&DRPC) will certainly involve a considerable amount of money in the form of a massive outlay and sustained budgetary allocation --- the bigger the budgetary allocation for it, the more extensive the coverage and the faster the process of eradicating poverty in the country. However, no consideration is big enough to overshadow the ultimate goal of the SEP(IDHC&DRPC), that is, to eradicate poverty by empowering the poor to break free from the prison of poverty through their own labour. Indeed, whatever amount of money put into the SEP(IDHC&DRPC) has every reason to be treated as investment expenditure proper and will, of course, be highly growth-positive for the economy in the short, medium and long run.

Given the huge size of Indian households living in poverty, India is not supposed to adopt or follow a piecemeal and half-hearted way of dealing the hydra of poverty. No matter how much money is shelled out every year for food and fuel subsidization, the Indian State cannot claim to have done its best against poverty just by preventing mass starvation. Moreover, as I touch upon at the beginning of this chapter, the country's mega-budget food guarantee schemes remain chronically affected by corruption at multiple levels. In spite of those mega-budget schemes formulated and launched in the name of the country's poor population but always ending up fattening the political class, bureaucrats and their agents in particular, we often come across heart-rending news of poor people dying of starvation in India, where a single family is permitted to live in a residential skyscraper reportedly worth over a mindboggling two billion USD!

Indeed, the very nature of India's anti-poverty programmes betrays the fact that the State lacks faith in the gigantic economic potential of its poor population. Apparently it considers the poor as an investment risk and does not, therefore, bother to think and come up with any big-ticket strategy for empowering them aggressively through intensive development of their human capital and systematic provision of physical capital so that they can come out of poverty and also climb up in the socio-economic spectrum not by means of the year-on-year dole but by virtue of their own labour.

In recent years, i.e. the current NDA innings, we have seen that the government has been channelling a great deal of resources into its 'Skill India' campaign. But I have my humble reservations about it having any significant impact on poverty, no matter what policy makers and their political bosses would often claim in their successive relevant policy papers and election manifestos respectively. One clear reason for my being sceptical about the much-hyped 'Skill India' campaign having any significant impact on poverty is the country's record of pathologically neglecting necessary follow-up measures. Our public toilets are a clear example of this peculiar national phenomenon. Our municipal authorities build a large number of public toilets. But as most of us must have observed with our own eyes, they are poorly maintained, if at all, with no proper supply of water, disinfectant or any other item indispensable for keeping them clean and safe. Likewise, a poor man may be skilled in a particular trade via the 'Skill India' campaign. But what use his newly acquired skill is actually of if he does not get a matching job or have the required minimum capital to start up and carry on the trade?

Even if the newly skilled man can go to a bank for a loan to buy his required minimum physical capital, he cannot, like any other poor person, be expected to be able to produce the required papers such as ITR's, PAN card and bank account statements, which any bank will necessarily demand, not to mention collateral. He may still have the option of approaching a local money lender or microfinance institute. But there too, he will be asked to produce many things that a poor person may not normally be able to; and there is no guarantee that the local money lender or microfinance institute will give him a loan only on the basis of his skill. Even if that happens, it will certainly be at a very high rate of interest, which can be as high as four times the average rate of interest charged by national banks. So the chances are that even after being skilled in a particular trade, say RMG-making, he may have no option but to take up whatever menial work is available to him until he actually lands a job in RMG-manufacturing or has somehow managed to acquire the required minimum physical capital to start up an RMG-making business.

If I may describe the 'Skill India' Campaign somewhat metaphorically, it is nothing more than training an army of people to fight and survive in the increasingly aggressive war of life but without providing them with the arms to actually fight and survive in it. So the 'Skill India' Campaign to be meaningful must be accompanied by a complementary programme to compulsorily provide all skilled persons with their minimum physical capital or suitable regular jobs.

But is being skilled and provided with the required minimum physical all that one needs to be able to successfully start up, run and sustain a business and also make it grow at a good pace? The answer is an emphatic no! If one wants and is also properly skilled to start a trade, say RMG-making, one must also be well acquainted with the general market conditions of RMG's and where to procure one's inputs from and sell one's finished products out for the right price. Moreover, one must possess at least some basic literacy and numeracy skills as well as sufficient knowledge about banking and finance. The logic is clear and simple. If the State's intent is to enable the poor to realize their economic potential to a satisfactory level and then transform them from a massive burden on the exchequer into productive and self-reliant assets of the nation, it must think beyond merely skilling them. In other words, the state must look at them through an all-encompassing lens and deal with them holistically. It is on the strength of this logic too that I have conceptualized and constructed the two-part framework of the SEP(IDHC&DRPC).

Owing to the need for the SEP(IDHC&DRPC) to cover a wide range of trades in demand and the unavoidably varying IDCH & DRPC costs of different trades, for example the IDCH & DRPC expenditure per direct beneficiary of garment-making will necessarily vary from that of carpentry or dairy farming, there cannot be a fixed budgetary allocation for every direct beneficiary across the board, implying that it is not practical to fix an IDHC & DRPC budget for a certain number of direct beneficiaries only on the basis of that number.

However, for the purpose of a broad analysis of budgetary considerations for the SEP(IDHC&DRPC), let me use the estimated average minimum IDHC & DRPC cost per direct beneficiary of five trades, viz. apparel-making, making of leather shoes and bags, local auto-rickshaw transport, carpentry and dairy farming, which works out at 1,16,000 INR. So if the target is cover ninety lakh eligible persons in the first year of its implementation, the required budgetary allocation is 1,04,400 crore INR --- 90 lakh direct beneficiaries multiplied by 1,16,000 INR --- exclusive of the outlay on establishing an implementing agency, raising a massive force of administrative and other personnel and setting up the required infrastructure as well as the cost of providing living allowances for them and their dependants. Is this too big an amount to be spent on empowering ninety lakh poor people directly and, by extension, their households to come out of poverty? No, it certainly is not!

Let me briefly discuss my reasons for that view. If the ninety lakh poor persons to be covered in the first year of its implementation are drawn from the country's ninety lakh poorest households, it does not take a lot of brain to conclude that their transformation into skilled and productive assets of the nation via the SEP(IDHC&DRPC) is bound to have a significant impact on their respective households too. Now going by the average size of

Indian households, which is about 4.9 members, the ninety lakh poorest households translate into 4.41 crore poorest persons, who will all be benefitted one way or another when one member of each of these households gets covered by the SEP(IDHC&DRPC). Indeed, the best part of the money to be spent on them will go straight into capital formation proper, while the rest will be spent on other heads such as compensation of the implementing agency's employees and living allowances for direct beneficiaries and their dependants. More precisely, an estimated 78% of the amount will be invested in long-term capital assets like sewing machines, auto-rickshaws and dairy cattle, all of which will steadily but surely contribute to the expansion of the economy in the long run.

If the general impact of the SEP(IDHC&DRPC) may be broadly analysed at household level, let me use the hypothetical case of a five-member rural household, composed of Mr. Tomba, his father, mother, wife and son, aged 34, 56, 55, 33 and 12 respectively. Assume that Mr. Tomba has undergone the IVGEP under the SEP(IDHC&DRPC) with RMG-making being his trade and been provided with the required physical capital like a motorized sewing machine, interlocking machine and iron, which are indispensable tools of RMG-making. Fresh from the IVGEP, if he manages to sew up only 3 formal shirts by working 8 hours per day, he may be said to generate a net value of 200X3=600 INR daily, based on current piece rates, which is, in other words, his daily income or value added. He can also increase his daily output by doing overtime without much hassle. So working 25 days a month, he can earn a monthly income of at lease 600X25=1,5000 INR in the first month, which is 6,801 INR in excess of the 2018–19 inflation-adjusted monthly cost of a basic living for a household of the same size, composition and setting, estimated at 8,199 INR (refer back to Chapter 1). Even if another 1,000 INR is added to the estimated monthly cost of a basic living for good measure, Mr. Tomba's household still has 5,801 INR left from his own income. This amount can now be saved in the form of an insurance policy, bank deposit, etc. for its own future. The same applies to all other direct beneficiaries and their households too. If they save even half their excess income and spend the other half on consumer durables and other household requirements, not only will the country's savings get boosted by a considerable amount but there will also be a steady improvement in the country's consumption/demand economics. Even in case of a drastic change in the assumed savings-consumption ratio, the economics of a country are always responsive to higher savings of or greater consumption by the poor. Indeed, the total monthly income of Mr. Tomba's household can actually be higher if other members in the working-age bracket --- his father, mother and wife --- are also engaged in some paid work, for example the MGNREGA work.

So Mr. Tomba and other direct beneficiaries of the SEP(IDHC&DRPC) will be able to offer qualitatively and quantitatively adequate food for their respective households as well as many other requirements of present-day existence. Even serious problems like hunger, malnutrition and stunting, which are rampant among the poor, will begin to ebb progressively as more and more poor persons get covered by it. Moreover, having undergone the IVGEP, they may be safely presumed to have gained a working level of knowledge about society in general, rights and responsibilities, personal and social values, health and hygiene and so on, and can, therefore, be expected to ensure that their parents and children are treated with due love and respect; that social welfare schemes are taken adequate and proper advantage of; that their children attend school regularly; that their constitutional rights are properly asserted and their constitutional duties properly discharged; and that a healthy way of life is lived. Altogether, their households are bound to undergo a significant all-round change for the better by virtue of whatsoever they will be gaining through the SEP(IDHC&DRPC) --- knowledge, skills, capital, etc.

It is also of relevance that their skills will progressively improve over time as they keep on using them. For example, they may be able to produce a certain amount of output per day in their initial days of production. But as their skills improve in terms of quality and speed, they will be able to get their respective trades down to a fine art, thus producing more and faster and better. Furthermore, they can transmit their skills to other household members so that the latter can also take part in the process of generating value, at least in some auxiliary capacity, if they are not otherwise engaged already.

To put it in a nutshell, the SEP(IDHC&DRPC) opens up a world of possibilities for Mr. Tomba's household or any other direct beneficiary's household, let there be no doubt. As more and more eligible persons get covered by it and transformed into productive units of the economy, their lives are sure to undergo a sea change in the right direction. When the overall conditions of more and more direct beneficiaries and, by extension, their households improve progressively through their own labour, the funding pressure of health care, employment guarantee schemes, food security schemes and the like on the country's exchequer is bound to ease up progressively. The improving financials of poor households also mean increasing demand for fast-moving consumer goods, durables like mobile phones and TV sets, and so on, which will, in turn, improve the income of manufacturers and help them achieve growth, notwithstanding the inflationary pressure of the progressive rise in general demand, which can, however, be kept in check through monetary policy interventions and by bringing about greater efficiencies in the utilization of the country's economic resources. The increasing income/profits of producers and manufacturers flowing from increasing sales will also lead to increasing tax collections for the government, though this explanation may sound a little too simplistic.

## THREE IMPORTANT QUESTIONS

Notwithstanding anything discussed and said above, three important questions about the practicality of the SEP(IDHC&DRPC) arise: First, is there enough budgetary room for the general government of India to fund as mammoth an additional anti-poverty programme as the SEP(IDHC&DRPC)?

Second, will its direct beneficiaries, whose trades involve production of one kind or another, be able to survive in the increasingly competitive production and marketing environment, which is, of course, dominated by super-sized conglomerates operating with considerable economics of scale and scope? And last but not least, what will be the actual impact of its implementation on the general demand and supply dynamics of those goods and services that will also be produced and provided by its direct beneficiaries?

As far as the first question is concerned, yes, spending 1,04,400 crore INR or so year after year on the SEP(IDHC&DRPC) until poverty is ultimately eradicated will, of course, be a major budgetary challenge. But let me also say in the same breath that it cannot be too big a challenge for the general government of a 3-trillion USD economy.

All the more so because 1,04,400 crore INR is only about 2% of the annual receipts of the central and state governments put together.

Indeed, the initial manpower-raising and capital outlay of the SEP(IDHC&DRPC) and its estimated first-year expenditure for 90 lakh direct beneficiaries could actually be less than the average amount of money annually forgone in the last ten years in the form of deep tax cuts and corporate interest waivers, which might have had the combined effect of cheering up India Inc and boosting investor sentiment at most. But it would not be wrong to suggest that instead of forgoing taxes and interest, if they had been collected and spent on something like the SEP(IDHC&DRPC), the economy would have witnessed a far better and bigger impact. What is actually needed for a country to be able to implement such a mega-budget anti-poverty strategy is a government that does not always look at the economy through the lens of the corporate world or act more like a corporate cheer leader all the time; and that not only has a very good sense of priority and equity but also exhibits it by way of policy measures.

The NDA government under the prime-ministership of Mr. Narendra Modi recently launched the National Infrastructure Pipeline, via which it plans to invest around 111 lakh crore INR on infrastructure in the next five years, i.e. by the end of 2025. It is a matter of national consensus that India as a major developing economy needs to invest heavily on its infrastructure to be able to grow quick enough. But by investing only about 10% of 111 lakh crore INR on the country's poor population within the framework of the SEP(IDHC&DRPC) in the next 10 years, India can bring about a transformational change in the general conditions of nine crore direct beneficiaries and their households, presuming an annual coverage of 90 lakh eligible persons.

Indeed, there are a few ways of raising funds for such a big-ticket programme as the SEP(IDHC&DRPC). One of them is to raise tax rates across the board, except those relating to goods and services mainly consumed by the poor. With a persistently low tax-to-GDP ratio estimated at a mere 11.30% in 2018, further down to 10.9% in 2019, India still has a lot of room to improve the ratio by raising tax rates and also expanding the tax base. It is important to note here that other developing countries have much higher tax-to-GDP ratios, with those of China, Brazil and South Africa estimated at 19.70%, 23.10% and 29.10% respectively. So India must also raise its tax rates progressively, particularly income and corporate tax rates, until its tax-to-GDP ratio rises to a reasonable level; and the resultant increase in tax collections can then be used to fund anti-poverty programmes like the SEP(IDHC&DRPC) and MGNREGA.

Furthermore, a cess on direct taxes for the purpose of raising part of the fund for implementing the SEP(IDHC&DRPC) can be introduced as provided for by Article 270 of the constitution of India. If the government does not want to resort to tax increases or cess imposition, it still has the option of funding the SEP(IDHC&DRPC) through additional borrowing, which is, however, not a very sensible one, though India still has a low overall debt-to-GDP ratio, estimated at 68.91% in 2018, compared to other major developing countries like China, whose overall (corporate, household and general government combined) debt-to-GDP ratio has already exceeded the 300% mark.

So raising tax rates, particularly direct tax rates, stands out as the most practical option if no significant changes are to be made in the present spending plans of the general government. If those who will be affected by the rise in their tax rates bother to analyse the general potential effects of the SEP(IDHC&DRPC) on the country's overall state of affairs, they will be able to conclude that it is not only the direct beneficiaries and their households that stand to benefit from the SEP(IDHC&DRPC), but also the nation as a whole. Let me explain this logic. From its launch, the SEP(IDHC&DRPC) will require a massive infrastructure and, therefore, be consuming a great deal of construction materials such as steel and cement, thus boosting their demand and production significantly. Also, if 90 lakh eligible persons get covered in the first year of its implementation, those who do not already own a mobile phone will be provided with one each, which means more business for the whole telecom industry. All of these will, in turn, lead to more profits for the companies involved, bigger pay cheques and perks, more jobs, fatter returns for investors and, of course, more revenues for the government.

And what does more money in the hands of the government mean? Of course, faster and broader infrastructure development, adequate funding for research and development, higher spending on national security and defence, higher social development spending and so on. Indeed, there will be an extensive multiplier effect of most spending on the SEP(IDHC&DRPC). So raising tax rates as a means of raising funds for it is definitely a practical option.

In recent years, politicians, former bureaucrats and renowned social scientists, particularly economists, have brought the idea of universal basic income into the national socio-economic discourse. For the Indian National Congress, presently the main opposition party, the *Nyuntam Aay Yojana or NYAY* (a universal basic income plan), is what can ultimately set the poor free from the bonds of poverty; and it formed an important feature of the party's manifesto vis-à-vis the 2019 Lok Sabha elections as well as a major electoral propaganda plan. The *NYAY* is intended to cover the 5 crore poorest households of India and guarantee them an annual basic income of 72,000 INR each at an annual cost of 3.6 lakh crore INR to the exchequer. This is, metaphorically explaining, nothing more than doling fish out to the poor households, when they are supposed to be trained in, and provided with equipment for, fishing themselves, which is the very logic underlying the SEP(IDHC&DRPC). The plan's acronym, NYAY, sounds pretty good, but then that is apparently all it has got to offer. With a similar annual budget, i.e. 3.6 lakh crore INR, the SEP(IDHC&DRPC) can be expected to lift all poor households of the country out of poverty in a matter of about 5 years. But the NYAY does not seem to envision poor households coming out of poverty. What it basically talks about is giving poor households money to live on year after year, sans any inbuilt incentive or plan for them to work their way out of poverty. So the NYAY's net outcome may not go much beyond prevention of hunger.

If the idea embodied in Step 3 in PART-II of the SEP(IDHC&DRPC) may be briefly reiterated here, there exists a great advantage of bringing it in over any other anti-poverty scheme in operation in India today. Though it is impossible to recovery the public money spent on most if not all anti-poverty schemes directly from their beneficiaries, the direct beneficiaries of the SEP(IDHC&DRPC) can be systematically incentivized to repay all or part of the money invested in them through it, their financials permitting, of course. For example, when a direct beneficiary manages to repay a minimum part or all of the money spent on him, he may be automatically given access to interest-free credit or even rewarded with a support package for expanding or upgrading his business.

Moving on to the second question, which is about survival of the direct beneficiaries of the SEP(IDHC&DRPC) in their trades in the face of increasing competition, it is quite obvious that being fresh entrants to their respective trades, they are bound to be confronted with multiple challenges in an increasingly competitive market environment, wherein big companies operate with sizable economics of scale and scope, and deploy advanced technology. However, there are a number of ways of enabling them to not only survive, but also operate profitably and sustainably. One such way is to require established companies, say major dairies such as Amul to procure milk in quotas from those direct beneficiaries who do dairy farming. Also, those direct beneficiaries trained in and provided with physical capital for RMG-making may be mostly geared up for export-oriented production. Indeed, there can be an integrated system of guided production and aided marketing and export for goods with potential surplus issues. The government can also seek to reasonably bend the internal rules of export in favour of the export-oriented direct beneficiaries.

Now the last question is about the potential impact of the SEP(IDHC&DRPC) on the supply and demand conditions of not only the industries concerned but also the economy as a whole. As the law of supply and demand basically says, a rise in the supply of a commodity with little or no change in its demand pushes its price down, thus affecting all along the general supply chain one way or another. So if, for example, its implementation creates another one lakh dairy farmers in India producing an additional 50 million litres of milk per month, the price of milk is bound to head southwards. This effectively means lower profit margins for the old milk producers in the country. The fall in their profit margins will, in turn, leave them with less money, which means they will then have to save and/or consume less than earlier. On the other hand, the new one lakh entrants to dairy farming will now be able to afford many new things for themselves, including what used to be afforded by old milk producers. So the fall in demand for goods by the old milk producers can be expected to be offset by the rise in demand by the new dairy farmers, who could not afford many things earlier. Moreover, the fall in the price of milk resulting from its additional production leaves more money in the hands of all its consumers, who can now purchase more of other things and/or save more money. If the supply of milk exceeds the country's effective demand for it, the excess supply can be exported not only in its natural form but also in the form of ice cream, milk chocolate, butter and so on so as to improve the country's balance of payments, though this is just a crude explanation.

As the SEP(IDHC&DRPC) is all about enabling the poor to come out of poverty by virtue of their own labour, its implementation is certain to transform them into an all-new class of consumers or a new all-round market that can absorb a significant part of the additional supply of goods and services resulting therefrom. Let me briefly expand on this theory. The new garment-making direct beneficiaries who could not afford milk for their households earlier will now be able to spare some of their income to buy it. Likewise, as if reciprocally, the new dairy farmers who could not afford adequate garments for their households earlier will now be willing and able to spend part of their income on new garments for their families. So part of the additional supply of a commodity, be it milk or garments, will certainly be consumed by the new class of consumers, who will also begin to demand previously unaffordable goods such as TV sets, motorcycles, skin cream and shampoo and services like private medical care and cinema. Overall, the implementation of the SEP(IDHC&DRPC) will certainly give a massive boost to the general supply and demand conditions of the economy as a whole.

## CONCLUDING REMARKS

On the strength of my own line of thinking about poverty eradication, which gets extensive expression in my formulation of the SEP(IDHC&DRPC), I feel it absolutely important to suggest that it must be incorporated into the country's socio-economic development framework as one of the pillars thereof. If implemented effectively and unwaveringly, it can not only transform the poor Bharatiyas of today into highly productive

Indians of tomorrow, but also turbocharge the conventional engines of the economy and help reverse the threatening phenomenon of ever-growing wealth and income inequality. Further, even after the poor population of the country have been freed from the prison of poverty, to the last man, the SEP(IDHC&DRPC) can still be pursued with some structural modifications so as to enable the households on the bottom rung of the socio-economic ladder to catch up with those on the higher rungs.

Lastly, let me touch upon the prominent potential effects of enabling the poor to come out of poverty via the SEP(IDHC&DRPC). As the poor embark on an economically productive and rewarding journey with a steady flow of income, they will all be gaining in their financial capacity to afford qualitatively and quantitatively adequate food and other basic requirements like clothing and toiletries and even personal transport. So their overall well-being will improve steadily. They will then be more willing to send their children to school and college in order for them to get proper education. They can also save part of their income so as to buy a TV set or a motorcycle, build a pucca dwelling, expand their business or meet their future exigencies. At national level, there will be a steady rise in food demand of the bottom of the social pyramid, accompanied by a steady fall in the incidence of health problems like anaemia, malnutrition and stunting among the poor, thereby bringing the cost of healthcare down. The country's life expectancy will be improving faster than usual. The school/college dropout rate among children, especially those belonging to the lower class, will be dropping steadily. There will also be a faster increase in demand for consumer durables and fast-moving consumer goods. Altogether, India will certainly emerge as a faster growing, more productive and richer economy and also a healthier and stronger nation in the wake of the introduction of the SEP(IDHC&DRPC), which must, therefore, be given enough thought and introduced and pursued on a military footing in the interest of socio-economic justice. In the interest of the poor and, by extension, the nation as a whole!

# Chapter Three

# TOWARDS TRANSFORMING THE PRISON POPULATION FROM LIABILITIES INTO ASSETS OF THE NATION

> "Prisons are out of public sight, and most often out of mind. But the vast majority of prisoners will at some point leave jail and rejoin our communities, which is why what happens inside matters to us all."
>
> David Lidington

Crime is a phenomenon that has not spared any civilization throughout the history of mankind. When the issue of crime ever arises, what usually springs to mind is the law, how well it has been enforced, what outcome it has yielded and so on. In our society, there is rather a reactive approach to crime that centers on a legal system resting mainly on penal provisions. Whenever a shocking crime takes place, the whole society tends to erupt into hue and cry, vehemently calling for the hanging and even public execution of the culprits, speedy enactment of tougher laws, brutal suppression of crime, etc.

The popular perception is that crime occurs because the existing law is not tough enough to deal with it. Thus, the national discourse on crime in this age of Twitter and Facebook gets dominated by this popular perception, with all intellectual and expert views lost in the babble. Sensing popular sentiment, our honourable lawmakers go on to pass tougher laws not because there is any scientific evidence or expert recommendations in favour of tougher laws, but primarily because it will invariably prove too costly in electoral terms to ignore popular sentiment in a democratic polity like ours.

The recent introduction of the death penalty for rape of girls under 12 years in consequence of a strong public reaction to the spurt of rape and murder of minor girls is a glaring example of this popular sentiment-driven trend in legislation. This is nothing short of dismissing the wisdom flowing from the vast literature on crime, being built up by various academic fields such as criminology, sociology and history, that however tough the law may be, it alone cannot prevent or control crime, as witnessed by the cases of rape taking place even in the immediate aftermath of the introduction of the death penalty for rape of minor girls under 12 years. Indeed, if draconian laws worked, there would be no crime in Saudi Arabia or Iran, where even theft convicts have to have their hands chopped off under the Islamic law of Sharia.

Causally linked to the negative side of the human character, the phenomenon of crime is bound to persist so long as mankind exists. However, the minimization of the incidence of crime has to be seriously pursued because crime imposes considerable costs on society as a whole. In order to bring the level of crime down, a holistic approach must be followed as the law is never enough per se to deal satisfactorily with it. In other words, every sphere of society has to play a role in handling crime. For instance, the corporate sector, through its Corporate Social Responsibility programmes, can make the unemployed youth job-worthy by skilling and upskilling them and also ensure them worthy jobs. This will help prevent the jobless youth from taking to criminal activities like theft, burglary and robbery, which are driven mainly by the socio-economic conditions of the youth involved. Indeed, this is the economic dimension of the phenomenon of crime, the main responsibility for dealing with which falls on the shoulders of the movers and shakers of the economic realm.

However, it is the education sector that must play a pivotal role in the fight against crime in the long run. Because education offers the best avenue of inculcating the young minds with the values that will gave them the moral capacity to exorcise the evils of greed, anger, hatred and the like from their own character. Unfortunately, those values are obviously missing in today's textbooks. So there is an urgent need to revise the curricula and syllabi of educational programmes in the country so that apart from knowledge acquisition, our children can develop a character of high moral standards through education. The idea is that future crimes can be effectively prevented in today's classrooms, provided that our children get the right blend of education.

It is often claimed that the criminal justice system in India, the land of the Mahatma, is more about reformation than vengeance. However, the validity of this claim stands invalidated by the very fact that the Indian law still provides for the death penalty when most democracies around the world have already abolished it. That said, the reformation-oriented measures being undertaken by the authorities concerned deserve mention and appreciation. The establishment of education and skill centres is one example. But the situation remains that a lot still needs to be done towards establishing and effective criminal reformation system through which the precious lives of those already trapped in the world of crime can be salvaged and transformed into responsible and productive assets of society.

The main theme of this chapter is about developing a reformation-oriented and productive ecosystem in prison wherein prisoners are exposed to reformation-oriented education and a disciplined way of life; their economic potential is systematically developed through a skill education programme; and they are also engaged in a productive process rather than rendering them idle throughout their imprisonment. It is true that convicts undergoing rigorous imprisonment and even some under-trial prisoners are allotted wage labour of one sort or another for which they are nominally paid. Indeed, they are not only underpaid but also mostly underemployed. This state of affairs needs an immediate review and must be corrected as soon as possible.

For the vast majority of the prison population who remain idle, indulging in bad pastimes becomes their default option of spending time in prison. To ignore this grim situation will be counterproductive, to say the least. Indeed, prison has become something of a safe haven for criminals, hardened or otherwise, to network with one another, establish new contacts and learn 'more effective and sophisticated' criminal tactics. Some prisoners exchange ideas about how to commit crime successfully. Some share their knowledge and experience about drug abuse. Some pick up nasty language and bad habits like chewing tobacco and smoking cannabis. All of these activities happen right under the nose of the jail administration, which is, in most if not all prisons, understaffed and cannot, therefore, be expected to look after every prisoner round the clock in mostly overcrowded jails. Under such circumstances, what should most of them be expected to be like when they get their liberty back? Is keeping them within the confines of prison the sole purpose of the law?

It is no secret that Indian jails continue to be governed under antiquated and retrogressive manuals containing several relics from the prison system of the colonial era. It is still a common practice of the jail administration to seek to control the conduct of prisoners and maintain a facade of discipline by treating them in a subtly degrading manner. Indeed, expediency takes precedence over compliance with established procedures, rules and rights when it comes to the treatment of prisoners in Indian jails.

Though there is a long list of shortcomings in the administration of prisons in India, as I have seen firsthand, it is not within the purview of this chapter to enumerate and highlight them.

Coming back to the main theme of this chapter, now let me ask how can an effective reformation-oriented prison system be set up? This is the question that this paper seeks to address. First of all, let us remember that when a man is born, his tabula rasa is just like an empty hard disk. As he grows up, his experiences in the external environment act like programmers writing programmes onto his hard disk. Now these programmes guide and control all his activities. But if a rogue programmer infects his system with a detrimental virus, say greed, the person starts thinking and acting irresponsibly and selfishly. The logic is that the social environment plays the principal role in the making of a man's character. As far as the reformation of a criminal is concerned, the challenge is to install a powerful anti-virus programme that has the capacity to eliminate virus-infected, or rather, crime-oriented programmes from his system or character. But unlike a virus-infected digital device, which can be disinfected in a matter of seconds using a powerful piece of anti-virus software, it will be a very challenging and time-consuming process to disinfect a crime-oriented character, which is, nevertheless, worth every effort.

If a suggestion may be put forward, the establishment of an effective criminal reformation system has to begin with a change in the attitude of society in general and the concerned authorities in particular towards criminals. No matter how heinous a crime a person may have committed, his/her commission of that crime does not change the reality of his/her being a human or diminish his/her human value. As a matter of fact, criminals are also social assets who have gone astray and turned liabilities owing to one social reason or another. When they get transformed back into law-abiding, responsible and productive members of society, they can and will doubtless contribute something to the overall progress of society. But if they are just left to rot in prison, it amounts to leaving some seeds of social progress to rot in vain. Can a civilized society ever allow that to happen?

Moving on to the question of transforming the existing prison system into a reformation-oriented one, it has to be recognized that there is a need to create a model prison manual in line with which all existing jail manuals must be amended so as to harmonize the administration of all prisons and ensure uniformity and equality in the treatment of prisoners throughout the country. When all prisoners are dealt with under the same law of the country, does it make any sense to treat them unequally? Though India has a federal structure of government, can the spirit of federalism be allowed to override the right of prisoners to equality before the law? In some prisons, inmates are served non-vegetarian diet periodically, whereas in many other prisons it is strictly prohibited. Some prisons provide inmates with telephone facility, whereas other prisons do not provide such an important facility. These are two examples of unequal treatment of prisoners, who are kept in prison under the same law.

The model prison manual must provide for three fundamental pillars on which a new structure of prison management may be built. They are Administrative, Correctional and Economic Branches, which are elaborated below.

i. **ADMINISTRATIVE BRANCH**

As the name clearly suggests, its responsibility is to deal with the administrative work of prison, which may be broken down succinctly as follows:

1. Entry of prisoners records and their proper keeping;

2. Enforcement and execution of court warrants/orders;

3. Escort arrangements for transportation of prisoners to and from courts/outside hospitals;

4. Provision of access to legal aid services, proper health care and welfare facilities;

5. Provision of other standard requirements of prisoners;

6. Maintenance of infrastructure;

7. Provision of internal and perimeter security: and,

8. Staff management.

These are the primary responsibilities to be taken care of by the Administrative Branch, which constitutes the linchpin and will also be superintending the two other branches. But it will not have a direct role to play in the process of transforming prisoners into law-abiding, responsible and productive citizens of the country.

ii. **CORRECTIONAL BRANCH**

It is this branch that is to be entrusted with the process of reforming the character of prisoners in an effective manner. The process should consist of two programmes, viz. Literacy and Numeracy Programme and Criminal Reformation Programme. Let me elaborate on them:

1. Literacy and Numeracy Programme

    The objective of this programme is to impart basic literacy and numeracy skills to all illiterate and innumerate prisoners. According to the National Crime Record Bureau data (2015), there are 1401 functioning jails in India with 414623 prisoners as on 31/12/2015, about 27% of whom are said to be illiterate. But there is no data on the innumeracy rate among the prison population, which must be a lot higher than the illiteracy rate. So a survey to identify illiterate and innumerate prisoners has to precede the initiation of the programme so that its overall requirements can be met in advance.

    It is said that the ideal duration of an adult literacy and numeracy programme consisting of 90 minutes of interactive classroom session and another 90 minutes of homework per day for six days a week is 3 months. As per the Right to Education norms, the ideal Pupil-Teacher ratio is 30:1. So going by this ratio, if a teacher conducts 3 90-minute classes per day for six days a week, he/she can impart basic literacy and numeracy skills to 90 illiterate and innumerate prisoners in a matter of 3 months. To cover about 1.08 lakh illiterate and innumerate prisoners at one go, 1200 teachers are needed. The issues of some illiterate and innumerate prisoners getting released before completing the programme and some illiterate and innumerate prisoners getting committed to prison in the meantime may arise.

Nothing can be done in the first case. But for newly committed illiterate and innumerate prisoners, they may be periodically enrolled for new batches of the programme.

As there are tens of thousands of graduate and postgraduate prisoners sitting idle in Indian jails, the teaching manpower required for the programme can be raised from among the prison population through a qualification test. It may be argued that these graduate and postgraduate prisoners, if without BEd/MEd, may lack teaching skills. But as the programme is all about imparting basic literacy and numeracy skills, it should not be a big deal for graduate and postgraduate prisoners to undertake the job. Moreover, a few domain experts may be roped in to groom them beforehand for the programme, for which they should also be paid as voluntary work beyond a certain limit becomes something of an imposition and will, therefore, affect the quality of its execution and outcome.

The programme is bound to impose an extra burden of finance on the prison department and, by extension, the government. Nevertheless, the potential costs are minuscule compared with the overall benefits, some of which are briefly discussed below:

a. It will keep enrollee-prisoners busy with learning, thus enabling them to channel their energy and time into as worthy and productive a process as learning and also preventing them from indulging in bad pastimes.

b. Learning is known to keep the brain healthy and boost memory and intelligence. It is also known to enable learners to better cope with mental health issues like stress and depression, which are endemic in prison. So keeping prisoners busy with learning can bring down expenditure on their mental health care in the long run.

c. When enrollee-prisoners successfully complete the programme, their newly acquired skills to read, write and do basic calculations are bound to not only instill a sense of satisfaction and confidence into them but also help them develop a sense of dignity and self-respect, which will, in turn, give rise to a sense of social responsibility in their psyche. Indeed, it is this sense of social responsibility that will set off the internal reformation process of the criminal mind. Such finer points are too important to be ignored when the goal is to transform criminals into law-abiding, responsible and productive members of society.

d. When over one lakh illiterate and innumerate prisoners become literate and numerate by virtue of the programme, it will be a major achievement as they will now be able to read and sign documents, forms, etc. instead of putting the thumbprint, do basic calculations, read newspapers, magazines and books and, therefore, understand entitlements, rights and responsibilities better. Indeed, it will be nothing short of empowering them for a better life. When they get reunited with the mainstream society after getting their liberty back, their newly acquired ability to read, write and do basic calculations will help them make good choices and decisions about life and society and become law-respecting, responsible and good citizens of the country in most if not all cases.

Given such significant benefits of imparting basic literacy and numeracy skills to all illiterate and innumerate prisoners, the Literacy and Numeracy Programme should be planned and launched without any hesitation or delay, whatever the financial costs. By the way, how can the government of a country with a $3 trillion GDP still leave millions of its citizens, prisoners or otherwise, illiterate and innumerate and allow them to live like Stone-Age people in this age of quantum computing, artificial intelligence and space travel programmes?

2. Criminal Reformation Programme

Crime has a number of social and personal factors, including the increasing disregard for moral values. Its incidence can also serve as a good barometer of the state of morality in society. There are several causes of the increasing disregard for morality and the resultant southward movement of moral standards such as social injustice, deprivation, inequality, lack of economic opportunities, lack of education and even public corruption. When such social evils become the order of the day, negative perceptions easily creep into social consciousness. Individuals who fail to rein in the flow of negative perceptions into their stream of consciousness usually end up committing criminal activities. But this is not necessarily the case of all criminals. There are also many criminals who commit crime not because of external factors but because of psychiatric disorders, inborn anomalies in their biological system, etc.

In most if not all cases of crime, perpetrators are motivated by wrong perceptions, which also erode their moral values. So the process of reforming criminals has to begin with correcting their wrong perceptions and boosting their morality. The main purpose of the Criminal Reformation Programme is to transform the character of criminals by bolstering their conscience and enabling them to rid themselves of antisocial perceptions and attain adequate standards of individual morality. As qualities like malleability and submissiveness are least likely to be found in the character of most prisoners, it will certainly prove quite challenging to influence their way of thinking about and understanding the world. But with the combination of multidisciplinary resources, to be drawn from relevant fields like criminology, sociology and psychology, it will certainly be practicable to right their wrong world view and give them the moral capacity to nip criminal propensities in the bud.

When prisoners get exposed to a well-designed series of powerful moral lectures full of edifying subject matter and also presented in a simple yet convincing manner, their outlook on life, philosophy and, by implication, character can be expected to undergo a significant change in the intended direction. Indeed, the subject matter should incorporate true and even fictional stories with a great deal of human interest so that they can help prisoners not only suppress negative feelings, impulses and inclinations but also develop a clean attitude to life with a sense of social responsibility. For example, a fictional story revolving around the brutal rape and murder of a woman on whom her aged parents completely depend for survival can be an effective medium for awakening and boosting emotional intelligence and empathy with the victim and her dependent parents. Moreover, the story should be presented in such an illustrative way as to enable prisoners to understand and feel every strand thereof without much difficulty. The narration of the story can be followed by an interaction between the lecturer and attending prisoners so that they can exchange their moral views arising out of and surrounding the story. Afterwards, the emerging individual views of randomly chosen attending prisoners can be systematically studied so as to assess the impact of the lecture.

The next session may present an analysis of the impact of drug-related crimes, for instance, heroin peddling, on society in a simplified but compelling manner with the help of a few case studies and hypothetical cases. It may begin with the hypothetical case of a local drug peddler, whose addicted customers include a 17-year-old schoolboy, who has now taken to stealing money from his parents so as to buy heroin and feed his addiction. The schoolboy has also come to neglect his studies, thereby putting his own future at risk. Making the situation even worse, he initiates some of his friends into heroin abuse. Now it may be presumed that his friends will also get addicted to heroin and then start stealing things, bunk off school and so on. They will also try and introduce some of their respective friends to heroin, resulting in a detrimental chain reaction, to which even the heroin peddler's own brother or son may fall prey someday. It is now quite clear how the lives of many can easily get sucked into the destructive chain reaction of drug abuse, set off by the self-seeking heroin peddler, who is driven solely by the lure of extraordinary profit. Following the presentation of the hypothetical case, attending prisoners should be encouraged to put themselves in the shoes of parents, brothers and sisters of those who get embroiled in the destructive chain reaction. Afterwards, they may be asked to express their honest views about drug abuse and peddling, which will provide the basis for further assessment of the impact of the programme.

In the following session, psychological techniques of beating criminal urges may be imparted to prisoners. As an example, the lecturer can use the hypothetical case of a delivery boy who is entrusted with the task of delivering a parcel to a flat. When he reaches the flat, he finds a lone, somewhat scantily clad young lady in a drunken state. His instant realization of the lady's undefended situation then triggers an animal desire in him. In such a slippery situation, what can enable him to suppress the immoral desire and prevent himself from committing a grave crime that may land him in graver trouble later? When confronted with such a situation, what he must instantly try and bring to mind is the nightmare that he and his family will go through in case his own sister or wife gets raped! The thought of his own sister or wife getting raped should be more than enough to send a chill down his spine, which will, in turn, help subdue the dangerous urge to take advantage of the lady's drunkenness and being alone. This psychological technique is about learning to think about and see the possible consequences of an action from both subjective and objective perspectives. There are also other psychological techniques that will, if mastered properly, enable anyone to resist any temptation to commit a crime or do something morally wrong. Such techniques have to be hammered into prisoners so that they can easily apply them to dealing with negative urges in the future.

Afterwards, there should be a lecture session that is centered around the fact that society is also a grand family, which relies for its existence and progress on the conduct of every member. Being members of society themselves, prisoners must be educated on the ancient Indian philosophy of *Vasudhaiva Kutumbakam* as well as social contract and its importance. Indeed, they must be convinced of the social responsibility to conduct themselves and work in the larger interest of society. But what if questions are raised about the prevalence of various social maladies like poverty, hunger, corruption, unemployment and increasing poor-rich disparity, which may be cited, though wrongly, as justification for flouting social contract and committing some forms of crime? The fact that crime actually aggravates such social maladies has to be driven home to prisoners by referring to a few relevant cases. To cite a hypothetical example, a poor man who desperately needs some money to get his broken-down auto-rickshaw repaired decides to steal something to sell and arrange enough money for the repair as no one has agreed to lend him the required amount. So he commits the criminal act of theft. But as in most if not all cases, the police catches up with him and he gets arrested for the crime. Now his poor family has no option but to sell off his auto-rickshaw so as to raise enough money to hire a lawyer to represent him in the court of law, to bribe the police not to torture him and so on. Moreover, his arrest means that he has to remain idle in prison until he gets released on bail or after getting acquitted or serving his sentence in case of conviction. Even after getting his liberty back somehow, his life may not be the same again because of social stigma of having been to prison, the sale of his only source of income, the auto-rickshaw, loss of respect, etc. So it may be concluded that the net outcome of his crime is the aggravation of his own misery. Another hypothetical example is that of the rise in the incidence of crime involving low-skilled workers like maids, drivers and watchmen because of which upper middle-class and affluent households become hesitant and unwilling to offer new jobs of the above descriptions, thereby damaging potential employment for unskilled and low-skilled workers. These two examples make it clear that crime does not pay, in most cases, to qualify a little. Nor does it help alleviate social maladies like poverty and hunger, which can actually get aggravated because of crime, as in the two above cases.

The last four paragraphs highlight some of my ideas about what should constitute the subject matter of lectures vis-à-vis the Criminal Reformation Programme. But more themes that could appeal to the conscience of prisoners must be explored and incorporated into the subject matter in consultation with domain experts. Also, more effective presentation techniques have to be deployed for better results.

In view of my first-hand experience and interaction with fellow prisoners over many years of my imprisonment, I am of the opinion that prisoners are not altogether bereft of conscience and morality. One strong piece of evidence of this proposition is that whenever the news of a heinous crime reaches the ears of prisoners, they can often be seen reacting in a unanimous manner that exhibits positive attitude and empathy with the affected people, say victims and their families. Let me cite a particular occasion when my fellow prisoners showed absolute unanimity in their reaction to one of the most abominable crimes of 2018. When a news channel broke the news of the brutal gang rape and murder of a minor Muslim girl in Kathua, J&K, it deeply shocked and saddened all of my fellow inmates tuning in to it, as I could easily judge from their angry frowns and murmurs. As the news got interrupted by a commercial session, they started making angry comments on the inhuman crime. The religious identity of the victim did not even matter, as witnessed by the fact that the angry comments cut across religious and racial lines. Interestingly enough, one rape accused, perhaps momentarily forgetting his own case, angrily commented that those who had committed the barbaric crime should be hanged in the public to serve as a strong deterrent. The spontaneous expression of shock and anger by my fellow inmates, including the rape accused, in reaction to the heinous crime is one crystal clear proof of the fact that criminals are not altogether devoid of conscience or morality. Indeed, being a criminal does not divest a person of human nature and there is always some room for their reformation. So it is very important for the authorities concerned to initiate the process of reforming prisoners by boosting the power of their conscience, inculcating them with moral values and giving them convincing reasons why they must never commit crime again.

Lecture sessions under the Criminal Reformation Programme must also be interspersed with brief talks on discipline, which needs to be promoted systematically in prison. Contrary to the common facade of strict discipline in prison, it is quite common for prisoners to conduct themselves in a manner that exposes a serious lack of discipline in prison. Indeed, they can often be seen threatening, abusing and even scuffling with each other, sometimes even in the presence of warders. It seems discipline, according to the jail authorities, is more about threatening prisoners with action and beating them actually and turning them submissive than about ensuring that they come to willingly conform to social norms and conduct themselves with the decencies of society. It may also be noted that there is no systematic approach to prisoners discipline. Whenever a discipline issue arises, for example, a scuffle between two prisoners, warders/head warders/officers on duty will respond by either rebuking or beating the prisoners involved. In some cases, prisoners involved may be put in solitary confinement for a certain period. That is apparently all what disciplinary action means to the jail authorities. Instead of following such a narrow reactive approach to prisoners discipline, if the inherent value of discipline is effectively communicated and driven home to prisoners, what will result in is a truly disciplined environment in prison, which will, in turn, facilitate the process of reforming them.

Discipline is not supposed to be construed only in terms of introducing and maintaining a set of rules. Just introducing some rules for prisoners and expecting them to blindly follow the rules will not lead to satisfactory compliance. If there is a rule for prisoners to strictly follow, there should also be a good explanation as to why they must follow it. For example, if a rule requires them to wash their hands with soap immediately before taking food, it is because doing so eliminates germs from their hands and prevents diseases like diarrhea and influenza. This is for the sake of their own health and so they will most likely be willing to follow it. Indeed, a proper explanation of what underlies a rule is certain to raise its compliance by far than without.

A few examples of rules that can form the foundation of discipline in prison are as follows, along with their succinct explanations:

a. Prisoners must not use offensive language or indecent innuendoes. Because the use of offensive words can not only corrupt the mind but also provoke anger, shame, hatred and the like, which will, in turn, lead to unwanted consequences like a shameful exchange of insults and even a physical fight, in which case the dignity of those involved is compromised.

b. Prisoners must not assault or scuffle with each other under any circumstances. Because violent conduct of any kind or extent not only goes against the very essence of what human nature should be but can also leave a dehumanizing impact on individuals involved. The fact that resorting to violent tactics is a disgraceful symptom of weakness should also be conveyed to prisoners. In case of a fight, the one who hits first must always be held mainly responsible for it and, therefore, liable to a heavier punishment.

c. All prisoners, regardless of their stature and status outside, must perform their personal chores on their own, such as washing clothes and doing the dishes. Indeed, there must be no *malik-naukar* or master-servant culture under the guise of *bhai-bandhi* or brotherhood and 'cooperation' among prisoners. Indeed, the common practice of the rich exploiting the poor happens in many ways in prison also. Prisoners with deep pockets mostly stay comfortably in prison, thanks to their poor counterparts who are usually at their beck and call to wash their clothes, do their dishes, massage them and so on in return for small favours like buying them a few packets of bidis and tobacco and giving them some money to meet other requirements. Rich prisoners, who usually enjoy jail officials' favour, are also smart enough to present their exploitation of poor prisoners as mutual assistance. But that does not change the reality. So how can the unfair dynamics between rich and poor prisoners be corrected? One answer is to instill a sense of humility into every prisoner and create an atmosphere of equal status among prisoners by requiring every prisoner to do their personal chores on their own and also perform their share of responsibility for keeping their respective wards/cells in hygienic conditions like sweeping and mopping the floor and cleaning the toilet. Indeed, every prisoner should be made to learn about and realize the importance and dignity of social labour the practical way. However, senior citizens and differently-able prisoners must be exempted so that the social responsibility to take special care of these two categories of people in all circumstances is always upheld and promoted even among prisoners.

d. Prisoners must strictly follow the following basic practices of personal hygiene:

- Washing the hands with soap immediately before taking food and after using the toilet;
- Brushing the teeth once in the morning and once before retiring;
- Clipping the nails once a week and getting the hair trimmed at least once a month;
- Avoiding unusual hairstyles and tattooing; and,
- Keeping bedding and clothing neat and clean.

As it is natural for every sane inmate to wish to be healthy and fit, they may be expected to fully comply with this five-practice rule for the sake of their own health, provided that they are properly educated on the importance of the above practices of personal hygiene citing relevant health tips. For instance, brushing the teeth once in the morning and once after supper ensures dental and oral health, which is essential for staying healthy and fit.

The introduction and enforcement of the above and similar rules will certainly improve the overall environment in prison and give prisoners a good understanding the importance of good conduct for both personal and social reasons. Once prisoners get accustomed to a highly disciplined environment in prison, it will naturally become easier for them to lead a socially acceptable and disciplined way of life after getting out of prison.

iii. **ECONOMIC BRANCH**

One of the primary reasons why India as an economy has failed to attain as much as it could and should, given its overall economic potential, is that it does not have a comprehensive human capital policy. The poor management of the country's human capital is clearly reflected in the way prisoners in Indian jails are treated, feeding lakhs of them, bearing the costs of their health care and providing them with their most basic requirements while the vast majority of them are not given the opportunity to even earn their keep.

According to the National Crime Record Bureau statistics, 2015 – the latest I have access to – the gross earnings through the production of goods by inmates trained in various vocational programmes were as high as 47.87 crore INR in Tamil Nadu with an inmates population of 14,122, thus generating 33,900 INR as earnings per head, whereas the corresponding figures of West Bengal were as low as 99.30 lakh INR, 21,523 inmates and 461 INR respectively. The huge differences between Tamil Nadu and West Bengal speak volumes for the gross underutilization of the human capital of prisoners in some states. When the highest earnings per inmate of 33,901 INR in Tamil Nadu is compared with the highest expenditure on inmates per head of 83,691 INR in Bihar, what comes to the fore is the fact that the prison population remain a major burden on the country's exchequer, thanks to the inability or unwillingness of the authorities concerned to systematically exploit the human capital of the prison population. So how can this sorry situation be reversed in the interest of the country?

First of all, a comprehensive profile of the human capital lying idle, underutilised or underdeveloped in Indian jails has to be drawn up. Then a framework for skilling and upskilling prisoners in India must be formulated on the basis of the profile. Though some jails do already have vocational training centres, their coverage in terms of prisoners and fields is too narrow. Moreover, most of these centres are run rather perfunctorily, in consequence of which most trainee-prisoners fail to attain an adequate level of expertise even on completion of whatever training they undergo. In view of their unsatisfactory performance, all the active vocational training centres will have to be shut down and replaced by Modern Skill Education Centres (MSECs), which must be established in accordance with the proposed framework.

**Modern Skill Education Centres**

The establishment of MSECs is the first step towards creating a productive ecosystem in each jail. It is through these MSECs that lakhs of idle prisoners can be skilled, upskilled and converted into economic assets of the country by grooming them according to modern skill requirements and providing them with employment afterwards through the creation of production units in jails.

As the Government of India has already launched a national skill education programme in the form of the Pradhan *Mantri Kaushal Vikas Yojna* (PMKVY), which is being implemented by the Ministry of Skill Development and Entrepreneurship through the National Skill Development Corporation, the MSECs can be brought within the purview of the PMKVY, which offers 219 courses on 32 sectors. But the MSECs should focus mainly on labour-intensive sectors like apparel and textiles, leather, furniture and handloom and handicraft. On completion of their respective skill courses, which must be in compliance with the National Skill Qualification Framework so as to ensure that the quality of training expertise that prisoners receive is actually up to the mark, prisoners should be provided with employment by setting up production units. Moreover, prisoners must be issued with a skill qualification certificate each as proof of skill qualification in the process of seeking employment after their release from prison.

**Production Units**

As prisoners graduate from the MSECs, it will be meaningless if they are not given employment in their respective areas of expertise. All the more so because their newly acquired expertise may well erode if not put into practice for long. It is, therefore, imperative to establish production units in prison and enable them to further hone their respective skills on the job by employing the in the actual production process.

The production units for manufacturing leather goods, pottery and ceramic products, furniture, textiles and apparel, etc. can be set up in jails. However, in view of the labour-intensive nature and market potential of the textile sector as well as the sector's global trends such as the falling share of China's exports caused by rising labour costs there and international trade conflicts, most prisoners should be skilled for the textile sector.

According to the IBEF data on the textile sector, the Indian textile market was worth around 150 billion USD as in July 2017 and is also projected to touch 250 billion USD by 2020. The new textile policy, formulated by the Government of India, also aims to achieve 300 billion USD worth of textile exports by 2025 and create an additional 35 million jobs, over and above the 45 million people already employed in the sector in question. So the human capital of the prison population must be effectively bolstered up and deployed in pursuit of these targets. Indeed, this is a great opportunity for establishing a productive ecosystem in each jail and enable the prison population to contribute to the growth of the Indian economy.

According to the National Crime Record Bureau, there are 134 central jails, 379 district jails, and 18 women jails in India, which are large jails with a capacity of over a thousand each in most of them. The rest are small jails, which accommodate small numbers of prisoners, as few as about 100 prisoners in many of them. In such small jails, it may not be practical to set up large production units involving economies of scale. So small production units requiring minimal physical capital, for example leather shoe-making units, may be set up in such jails. However, large jails accommodating over one thousand prisoners each should have large production units so that the advantages of scale can be taken.

**Bringing India Inc on Board through Corporate Social Responsibility**

In the process of boosting and exploiting the human capital of the prison population in the interest of the economy, India Inc, i.e. the corporate sector, can play the main role via the Corporate Social Responsibility (hereafter referred to as CSR) provisions under Section 135 of the Companies Act, 2013, according to which companies with an annual turnover of 1000 crore INR and more or a net worth of 500 crore INR and more or an annual net profit of 5 crore INR and more shall commit at least 2% of their average net profit in the previous three years to CSR activities.

With a least 6,000 companies falling within the ambit of the CSR provisions, generating a corpus of over 20,000 crore INR, some major companies can be brought on board to undertake CSR activities in jails across the country. Indeed, creating a productive ecosystem in each jail through the CSR provisions will be a lot easier and more efficient than bringing about the same by depending entirely on the government for budgetary allocations, among other things.

For some companies, the whole process can throw up opportunities for horizontal expansion of capacity by outsourcing the manufacturing of their low-end products to production units in jails at comparatively low labour costs. For production units in jails, being associated with big companies will certainly boost the marketability of their products. Thus, it will be a win-win situation for all involved, not to mention its potential socio-economic impact.

**Analysis of Socio-economic Impact**

Apart from being a source of income, employment gives dignity and a sense of responsibility to those who are qualified and fortunate enough to have it. Indeed, employment plays a major role in promoting social stability, security, cooperation and progress. When prisoners are also provided with employment by establishing a productive ecosystem in each jail, what will arise is a virtuous circle which will massively impact society in a very positive manner. The most immediate effect of prisoners being engaged in a productive process rather than rendering them idle is that they will no longer have enough time to indulge in detrimental habits such as gossiping about others and smoking cannabis in groups, which badly affect both the body and mind. They will also have a steady flow of income from employment, which will enable them to deal with a number of issues that usually arise and confront prisoners, especially those who are poor.

In pursuing their respective cases, a large number of prisoners depend on state-appointed counsels, who tend to work on their own terms, leading to inordinate delays in disposing of cases and appeals as well as to the increasing legal pendency rate. As there is a common, not entirely unfounded, perception among prisoners that state-appointed lawyers do not handle cases earnestly enough, most prisoners will not hesitate to hire lawyers on their own, provided of course that they have the financial means to do so.

Indeed, with a regular flow of income from employment, they will be able to contract lawyers on a pay-per-hearing basis and dictate terms to them. If the lawyers fail to live up to their reasonable expectations, prisoners can fire them at will. The likelihood of getting fired for underperformance is bound to put pressure on lawyers to study a lot, work harder and perform better to be able to survive in the increasingly competitive litigation market. Then what can be expected to ultimately arise is a fairer, more balanced and efficient legal environment.

Moreover, when prisoners begin to pay lawyers with their hard-earned money, not only will state expenditure on providing legal aid services to prisoners come down but they will also come to regret whatever crime they may have committed in consequence of which they now have to spend their labour money pursuing their respective cases.

Among the prison population are tens of thousands of extremely poor prisoners, many of whom are also the sole breadwinners of their respective families. Owing to their imprisonment, their families are now in dire straits. The education of their children is badly affected. Their families can no longer afford adequate food. Indeed, it is their dependent innocent children, wives and aged parents who mainly bear the brunt of their imprisonment. But if and when these poor prisoners are skilled and then engaged in a productive process and have a steady flow of income, they will be able to mitigate the adverse effects of their imprisonment on their respective families by supporting them financially from inside prison.

It is true that the jail administration provides prisoners with some bare essentials, which are, however, hardly adequate to ensure them an easy and proper existence in prison. So they depend on their respective families for all other basic requirements such as undergarments, towels and slippers, which are not issued by the jail authorities. Moreover, their families have to give them some pocket money regularly so that they can buy small necessary items available at prisoners welfare canteen. Altogether, it is a financial burden on their families, particularly those belonging to poor and lower middleclass categories. However, being engaged in paid employment in prison will enable prisoners to meet all their personal requirements on their own, thus ridding their respective families of the burden of having to support them financially. Even those poor prisoners who get no family support at all will no longer have to remain barefoot or manage without adequate clothes once given a steady source of income with which to meet at least their minimum essentials.

Furthermore, prisoners, particularly convicts, must be encouraged to save part of their income regularly so that they can raise enough savings to build their new lives on and turn over a new leaf after getting them to subscribe to the National Pension Scheme. Such a measure will certainly give them confidence and guarantee a better future for them.

As briefly stated above, the textile sector offers a huge export potential. Furthermore, it is a highly labour-intensive sector. So large- and medium-scale production units for manufacturing textile goods must be set up in jails so that most prisoners can be provided with employment once they finish their skill education. When these production units start manufacturing textile goods, the country's overall textile production will get boosted, which will, in turn, lead to higher textile exports and greater inflow of dollars, thus tiding the economy over the chronic issue of the current account deficit.

It cannot be doubted that bolstering up and utilizing the human capital of the prison population systematically will certainly contribute to the country's economic growth, even if by a small fraction, and incorporate tens of thousands of poor countrymen into the growth process of India as an economy.

The multiplier effects of establishing a productive ecosystem in each jail and providing prisoners with paid employment are also worthy of a brief analytical reference here. It is an undeniable fact that most if not all prisoners consume less than they normally should and would like to because of many constraints, their lack of financial means being the biggest one. But with a steady flow of income they will be willing and able to increase their overall consumption. Let me cite the hypothetical case of an idle prisoner. Owing to lack of financial support from his family, the idle prisoner buys only a cup of tea per day from prisoners welfare canteen. But following the initiation of a textile skill training programme, he undergoes a skill training in RMG-making. As he finishes the skill training programme, an RMG-making unit also gets established in jail, where he gets a job earning him 5,000 INR a month. So he now decides to buy two cups of tea per day. Under similar circumstances, if one lakh prisoners decide to double their daily consumption of tea, or any other item, for that matter, there will be a significant increase in demand for tea and other basic ingredients for making tea such as milk and sugar as well as accompaniments to tea such as biscuits and cakes. The increase in demand for these goods drives the relevant industries to ramp up production, which means more inputs, including labour. It is now clear that providing prisoners with a regular source of income will bolster up the demand for many goods needed by them, which will consequently mean higher production and income for the relevant industries. Moreover, higher income will generate higher tax revenue for the government. Altogether the nation stands to greatly benefit from investing in and utilizing the human capital of the prison population. So what are the authorities concerned waiting for?

## CONCLUDING REMARKS

Crime is an incurable social disease, from which the human world has been suffering throughout its existence. So the primary question about crime should be, how can its growth be stemmed and its incidence then minimized so that it does not drive society into a chaotic and lawless state of affairs? In the case of India, crime is primarily handled through penal provisions and the criminal reformation part is conspicuous by its near absence. A broad analysis of Indian crime statistics (2006–2015) reveals that nearly 75% of crimes, mostly theft cases, that took place in the same period were committed by persons with at least one criminal case each already registered against them. In other words, most crimes between 2006 and 2015 were committed by previously arrested suspects and habitual offenders. This obviously means that there is a pressing need to pay enough attention to the reformation and rehabilitation of criminals if crime is to be dealt with effectively enough.

What this paper propounds are some important reasons why the prison system in India should be reformed and rebuilt on the three fundamental pillars of (i) Administrative Branch, which is to manage the general administrative work, (ii) Correctional Branch, which is to be entrusted with the responsibility of transforming the character of prisoners via Literacy and Numeracy Programme and Criminal Reformation Programme, and, (iii) Economic Branch, which is to bolster and utilize the human capital of the prison population through the establishment of Modern Skill Education Centres and production units in each jail/correctional home. Only when prisoners are systematically transformed from liabilities into responsible and productive assets of the nation, will it be within the realms of possibility to bring about a steady fall in crime, which will, in turn, lead to the following outcomes, among other desirable changes in society:

1. More stable and secure socio-economic environment;
2. Lower expenditure on policing and maintenance of law and order;
3. Steady drop in the rate at which new cases get registered and referred to courts, thus giving the already overburdened judiciary more room to handle and clear adjudication backlog and improve the quality of justice; and,
4. Steady fall in the prison population, which means lower budgetary requirements for jails.

Lastly, I would like to recommend all concerned about criminal justice, reformation and rehabilitation to sometimes think over Oscar Wilde's quote that goes, "The only difference between the saint and the sinner is that every saint has a past, and every sinner has a future", which also evokes the great transformation of Shri Ratnakara from an evil and dreaded dacoit into a great saint, who went on to author the Ramayana! Let me conclude this paper by dedicating my poem "From Darkness to Light" to every prisoner the world over:

## FROM DARKNESS TO LIGHT

Oh less fortunate rower of life!
Alas, you have been thrown adrift
Into the sea of darkness teeming with black sharks
By the irresistible waves of greed, passion or perception.

But you are still in the precious raft of life force,
A reason big enough to look on the bright side.
Indeed, life is unwilling to give up on you yet,
Expecting you to start living up to its expectations someday.

So with a deep inhalation of hope and positivity,
Take up the oars and go on to row the precious raft valiantly,
Rising above the crest of the strong waves
As you negotiate them, one after another.

Even if darkness disheartens and disorients you
As you endeavour to navigate your route,
Stick to the needle of the moral compass
As it always points in the direction of light.

The weather may be unforgiving and even arbitrary at times,
Putting you through gale, hail and rain.
But once you let your innate grit take over,
No odds are too overwhelming for you to overcome.

The inescapable lighthouse of justice also stands tall there,
Not only offering you a bright passage
And guiding you through the route you deserve,
But also seeking to salvage your enmeshed life.

So row and row forward grittily
Until you reach the shore of light,
Where a new dawn of life awaits you
With the whole world waiting to welcome you back.

***

# Chapter Four

# PUTTING GOLD IN THE DOCK FOR ROBBING MANKIND

> "(Gold) gets dug out of the ground in Africa, or someplace. Then we melt it down, dig another hole, bury it again and pay people to stand around guarding it. It has no utility. Anyone watching from Mars would be scratching their head."
>
> **Warren Buffet**

At some point in time, we have all heard about humans robbing gold. But this chapter sheds some light on the presence of a diametrically opposite phenomenon, or more precisely, how and what gold has actually robbed not just some people but the entire human race of!

Nobody knows for sure since when humanity has been in misplaced love with gold. If some historical treatises are to be believed, gold first came to be used in medicine by Chinese physicians about 2500 BC for treating diseases like smallpox and skin ulcer. But the first firm archaeological evidence of man's interaction with gold suggests that it occurred in ancient Egypt circa 3000 BC. So it can safely be concluded that man had discovered gold at least 5000 years ago.

According to the World Gold Council, the quantity of gold mined throughout history is 197,576 metric tons, which is worth about a mind-boggling 988 lakh crore INR as on 04 June 2021 or about 13.17 trillion USD at the current exchange rate, or about 14.20% of the world's GDP. It is also about double the conservatively estimated budget for the One Belt One Road initiative of China, the single largest international connectivity project that the world has ever witnessed. If the amount is equally distributed among the world's population, every person gets a little over 1,667 USD or about 1,25,025 INR. But if equally distributed among the bottom billion of the human race, each one of them gets 13,170 USD or 9,87,750 INR and poverty just disappears off the face of the earth.

It is no exaggeration to say that 13.17 trillion USD is more than enough to bring about a big-bang transformation on a global scale. If I may list some super-massive projects that can be executed with this humongous amount of money, which remains buried in the grave of gold, they are as follows:

1. Construction, running and maintenance of 50,000 well-equipped general hospitals with 50 beds each at an estimated total cost of 50 billion USD.

   Impact Assessment:

   a. Improvement in the global availability of hospital beds by 1 per 3,160 persons;

   b. Easier and faster access to health care facilities;

   c. Better intervention in health issues; and,

   d. Significant reduction in disability-adjusted life years (DALYs) and socio-economic costs of health problems.

2. Incremental construction, running and maintenance of 10 lakh modern schools, 25 thousand modern engineering, medical, nursing and general colleges and 1 thousand state-of-the-art universities at an estimated total cost of 2.8 trillion USD.

Impact Assessment:

a. Universal access to education;

b. Widespread development of human resources;

c. Higher economic productivity; and,

d. Better social dynamics and environment.

3. Construction and maintenance of 15 lakh kilometers of green-field, standard two-lane tarmacked road, 1 lakh kilometers of standard broad-gauge railway lines and 25 thousand high-speed railway track, along with thousands of bridges and their supporting infrastructure, especially in backward regions of the world at an estimated total cost of 2.90 trillion USD.

Impact Assessment:

a. Better land connectivity across backward regions;

b. Higher efficiency in transportation;

c. Boosting economic activity across the world; and,

d. Higher socio-economic interaction among different regions.

4. Construction and distribution of 20 crore low-cost smart concrete homes among the poorest of the world's population at an estimated cost of 2.5 trillion USD.

Impact Assessment:

a. Eradication of homelessness;

b. Improvement in the living conditions of the poor; and,

c. Social equity.

5. Construction, operation and maintenance of as many wind, solar and hydroelectric power plants as required to generate

500 GW of renewable energy at an estimated cost of 1.60 trillion USD.

Impact Assessment:

a. Universal access to energy;

b. Significant fall in the global consumption of fossil fuel; and,

c. Considerable slowdown in anthropogenic climate change.

6. Establishment of 500 advanced research and development institutes for medical and agricultural sciences, with state-of-the-art facilities at an estimated overall cost of 250 billion USD.

Impact Assessment:

a. Better management of medical challenges thrown up by endemic, epidemic and pandemic diseases;

b. More effective handling of agricultural challenges arising from the world's population growth, climate change, deterioration of soil health, etc.;

c. Higher per capita availability of food and prevention of hunger and malnutrition; and, healthier global population and resultant fall in health care budget across the world.

7. Establishment of 10 lakh small- and medium-scale corporative business enterprises for the poor at an estimated cost of 500 billion USD.

Impact Assessment:

a. Mass employment for the poor;

b. Higher standards of living among the world's poor population;

c. Prevention of hunger and undernourishment among the poor population; and,

d. Higher growth rate of the world's GDP.

8. Construction, operation and maintenance of 25 thousand agricultural dams and 50 lakh kilometers of mid-width concrete agricultural irrigation channels at an estimated cost of 600 billion USD.

   Impact Assessment:

   a. More efficient water management;

   b. Higher production of food grains per unit of expenditure and subsequent fall in the agricultural price level; and,

   c. Eradication of hunger and undernourishment.

9. Initiation of global adult education programme so as to impart literacy and numeracy skills and basic knowledge of life with a total budget of 250 billion USD.

   Impact Assessment:

   a. Empowerment of the global masses by ensuring that every person has the basic knowledge of life and abilities to read and write and do basic calculations; and,

   b. More developed human capital of the world population.

10. Plantation of 1 trillion trees worldwide at an estimated cost of 1.5 trillion USD.

    Impact assessment:

    a. Cleaner and healthier global environment;

    b. More effective management of flood and water resources;

c. Controlling global warming; and,

d. Easier conservation of wildlife.

So the grand total of the above estimated costs stands at 12.95 trillion USD, which is still about 220 billion USD short of the total estimated current value of the world's gold ever mined. The estimated individual project costs were not plucked out of the air; they were calculated on the basis of the prevailing cost conditions in India. Refer, for instance, to the connectivity projects involving 15 lakh kilometers of green-field, standard two-lane tarmacked roads and 25 thousand kilometers of high-speed railway track. Indeed, their estimated separate costs were worked out on the basis of the estimated costs of projects under the *Bharatmala Pariyojana* and Ahmedabad-Mumbai High-Speed Rail project.

Now, just think about the big-bang transformation that will ultimately result from those listed projects, which can be carried out with the amount of money that the world has sunk in the yellow 'zombie' asset. In terms of employment generation, what will directly arise from those projects are hundreds of millions of long-term jobs for doctors, nurses, teachers, professors, etc. and short-term jobs for construction workers, machine operators, etc. Apart from that, millions of more jobs will be created indirectly. For example, the projects are bound to greatly boost the global demand for building materials like cement and steel, implying more jobs in these sectors.

On the other hand, only about 9.3 million people are presently employed worldwide in industries centring around gold, primarily the gold jewellery sector, with India having an estimated 5 million people employed in this industry in 2020 (IBEF report), distantly followed by China with about 1.3 million people employed in it. It includes about 0.25 million people directly employed by gold-mining companies, around 19 thousand people directly employed by central banks around the world to deal with their gold reserves and about 0.35 million persons employed as security guards at official gold vaults, jewellery shops, etc.

As the 10 listed mega projects get into implementation, the world's GDP will get boosted by more than the amount of dollars getting committed to them annually through the multiplier effects. As people getting employed under the above projects will begin to enjoy a regular flow of income, they will, of course, be spending part of it, which will, in turn, become income for others, who will also be spending part of their income, resulting in the multiplication of the initial spending. The same is true of those industries that will be supplying construction materials to the projects. For example, if the projects buy 50 billion USD's worth of cement, the cement industry will most likely be spending part of it on capacity expansion, acquisition of new limestone quarries, etc., which will then become income for others and so on. The cycle continues until the spending portion diminishes to zero at some point down the spending chain. Thus, the projects will lead to the expansion of the world's GDP by more than their actual values put together.

But, unfortunately, man, the most intelligent being on earth, has allowed himself to be robbed of all those great possibilities by gold, the inanimate shiny robber, thanks mainly to its rust-proof nature and seductively shiny quality, which appeals to the irrational side of man, reflected primarily by the extravagant and frivolous aspects of his culture and religion. Furthermore, millions of cases of crime like smuggling, snatching, fraud, robbery, burglary and even murder revolve around gold, thereby causing a great deal of loss and suffering to the victims. Altogether, gold has been an irresistible evil for mankind!

It is true that gold has many practical applications as in orthodontics and other health care areas because of its biocompatibility, in electronics because of its high conductivity and malleability and even in space suits and vehicles because of its good reflectivity. But one estimate suggests that less than 10 thousand metric tons of gold will be required to meet such uses in the next thousand years, also with gold being steadily substituted with other cheaper but equally or more useful metals, if the amount of gold used in electronics is recycled and, of course, no other practical applications of gold emerge in the meantime. In other words, the world has already accumulated nearly 20 times more gold than required for all known practical purposes in the next thousand years! This seems like a sheer madness. All the more so because hundreds of millions of fellow humans continue to live in extreme poverty across the globe today!

Coming back to India, it is not for nothing that India is called the *perennial sink* of gold. According to the World Gold Council, India has a conservatively estimated 26,000 metric tons of gold, which is currently worth about 130 lakh crore INR, that is, almost the country's estimated COVID-hit GDP of 2020–21. Indeed, this is more than the amount of money required to solve most intractable socio-economic problems confronting the country like poverty, hunger and homelessness. But who is really bothered about such problems except those actually affected by them?

Over and above the amount of gold already hoarded in India, the country continues to import hundreds of metric tons of gold every year. In 2018 alone, the amount of gold imported was 759 metric tons, which is, however, 15% lower than the previous year's because of the imposition of higher import duty and GST at 10% and 3% respectively. Then in February 2021, import duties on gold got cut down to 7.5%, though a 2.5% cess was introduced.

The World Gold Council claims that 75% of India's gold demand is from the jewellery sector. With over 50% of its population under 25 years, more than 50% of India's gold demand for gold is generated by weddings, with a major part of it going into the tradition of giving dowries. Out of the total quantity of gold imported in India, at least 20% has to be exported back as required by an RBI rule intended to help tide the economy over the yawning CAD. This means that a sizable amount of India's gold import finds its permanent home in the country, causing a regular outflow of foreign exchange.

When it comes to the smuggling of gold into India, there are a number of conflicting reports as to the quantity. Some claim that the actual quantity of gold smuggled into the country is in the range of 30–50 metric tons, whereas others put the figure at well over 100 metric tons. In April 2014, P. Chidambaram, then Finance Minister, revealed that gold smuggling had touched 3 metric tons a month, which sounds like a gross underestimation compared with the World Gold Council's estimate of a whopping 150–200 metric tons per year. In his article, *What makes India a gold smuggling destination?*, published in *indiatoday.in* on 13 July 2020, Prabhash K Dutta writes that though India's annual consumption of gold is about 1000 metric tons, but India imports only about 800 metric tons of the yellow metal, implying that 200 metric tons of gold gets smuggled into the country every year. This implication is in agreement with the World Gold Council's estimate of the quantity of gold smuggled into India.

It has to be noted that gold smuggling is not actually as highly profitable a way of making money as generally perceived. Averaging the profit margins claimed by a few persons involved in gold smuggling through Myanmar, Nepal and Bangladesh, including some of those who were arrested in connection with gold smuggling and imprisoned, it is found that a smuggler makes about 6 lakh INR per kilogram of gold. What surprises me is the fact that it is still possible to make a negligibly lower profit by importing gold through the legal and proper route. So why smuggle gold with all those associated risks? There are a few possible explanations for it. Black money arising out of political and bureaucratic corruption, tax evasion, illegal mining, drug smuggling, etc. is getting laundered by smuggling gold and putting it into the growing jewellery sector by means of fake invoices with the connivance of major jewellery companies. Moreover, black money can be conveniently used to buy gold on the black market. Then the yellow metal can be stashed away as long as needed without the risk of getting affected by inflation or demonetization. So this means that plus-minus 1 lakh crore of mostly black money gets converted into gold through smuggling every year! How's the josh?

According to an Indian Chamber of Commerce report, '*India's Gold Rush: Its Impact and Sustainability*', the value of gold imports throughout the years of slowdown (2005–2012) was higher than the country's expenditure on urban development, health, education, housing and family welfare taken together. This fact speaks volumes about the country's blatantly skewed priorities at various levels. Another interesting fact is that over 30% of the world's annual gold production, which was 3200 metric tons in 2020, ends up in India, though its share of the world's GDP stands at barely 3.5%. This also contributes greatly to India's trade deficit, which was 157.50 billion USD in 2020 and makes it a tougher to become a stable CAS economy. Moreover, India's share of the world's private holding of gold is about a mind-boggling 40%, which is outlandishly out of proportion!

Given the huge private gold holding of India, the Government of India launched the Gold Monetization Scheme in 2015 with the aim of mobilizing the gold holding of households and institutions in the country. But the scheme has failed to take off and so gold remains a big drag on the productive process of the Indian economy, which is, however, projected to recover from the COVID-driven slump with a estimated growth rate of 10.5% (RBI) this fiscal year(2021). Also, social realities like the lack of financial literacy among the vast majority of the Indian population and the strong bond between gold and the Indian culture are further complicating the sorry state of affairs involving the shiny metal. That Indian households today park over 70% of their savings in gold and real estate is a clear symptom of the gold obsessive disorder, which India acutely suffers from. Curing the country of this disorder will certainly be a big challenge involving radical policy reform.

It is true that gold has been on a bull run since 1998, outperforming fixed deposit and interest rates offered by banks.

But if we look at the returns trajectory of the Indian stock market, it can be seen that the rate of returns from investment in the Indian stock market in the last two decades has been more than double the rate at which the value of gold has grown in the corresponding period. Moreover, gold jewellery, in which most Indian households invest, does not fetch its real value at the time of liquidation, resulting in a further loss of returns from holding gold for them. So it can safely be concluded that there is not much prudence in Indian households' investment in the yellow 'zombie' asset.

Going by some data drawn from the 68$^{th}$ Round of NSS on gold consumption in India, the monthly per capita expenditure of the richest 5% of the Indian population on gold ornaments is 249.95 INR, whereas the corresponding figure of the poorest 10% is a miniscule 0.21 INR! The two comparative statistics show that it is the rich who are directly responsible for the great Indian gold conundrum. Today about 130 lakh crore INR has been driven out of the economic process of India mainly through the hoarding to thousands of metric tons of gold by the superrich. This reality is also an indubitable testimony to the incoherent and unsustainable gold policy of India. But being a capitalist democracy in reality, as opposed to what has been envisioned in the Constitution of India, the country's political leadership cannot afford to bring about a radical policy change mainly because of electoral considerations.

The gems and jewellery sector, which consumes most if not all of the gold imports, contributes 7% or so to the GDP and about 15% to the total merchandise exports. Though the same round of National Sample Survey estimates that 20.8 lakh persons were employed in the same sector, an IBEF report now claims that over 46.4 lakh persons are currently employed therein. However, the role of the sector in creating jobs cannot be a justification for the government to put up with the constant hoarding of gold by the affluent class. It should also be noted that it is the part of cut and polished diamonds that constitutes the largest share of the exports from the gems and jewellery sector. Out of the total gems and jewellery exports between April and August 2018, which stood at 13.18 billion USD, cut and polished diamonds were worth 10.31 billion USD, i.e. a whopping 78.22% in value terms. This obviously means that it is only a small fraction of the total gold imports that gets exported in the form of jewellery, with the rest actually adding to the continuous build-up of the yellow 'zombie' asset in India, about 22% of whose population or roughly 269 million Indians live below the poverty line, as stated by the Government of India in 2012. If half the build-up of gold in India is liquidated and its proceeds are channeled into the productive processes of the Indian economy , jobs can be created not in lakhs but in crores and various socio-economic maladies like hunger, homeless and unemployment can also be dealt with by far more effectively.

Indeed, gold is nothing short of an irresistible prostitute whose rust-proof nature and ageless shine constantly seduce man into demanding more and more of it. As the world keeps on demanding more and more of the yellow metal, it keeps on robbing the human race of more and more of its economic potential by sucking up hundreds of billions of dollars year by year, which, if systematically diverted into other productive processes of the world's economy, would certainly have created millions of jobs, bolstered up the combined GDP of the world, freed millions of people from the clutch of poverty, prevented hunger and malnutrition and made the world a better place by far!

In view of the above facts and figures, let me put it to you, even if metaphorically, that gold is the biggest robber of all time! So the question now is, how can this robber be brought to justice? The best answer is, I believe, for all the governments of the world to compel their citizens by law to hand this metallic robber over to them in return for adequate rewards and convert it into something that can be sold, bought and possessed by sovereign governments only. Moreover, so as to meet the practical requirements of gold, governments can follow a quota mechanism for gold, including for the purpose of electro-plating jewellery and other things, which may be needed from an aesthetic point of view. Indeed, I would love to comprehensively expand on this answer but in another paper on the same topic.

# Chapter Five

# THE EXTRAVAGANT PRACTICES OF HINDUISM AND THE CONCEPT OF ECONOMICAL PIETY

> "The problem with religion, because it's been sheltered from criticism, is that it allows people to believe en masse what only idiots or lunatics could believe in isolation."
>
> **Sam Harris**

Even in this age of artificial intelligence, quantum computing and space travel, religion continues to occupy a great deal of space in the world. Hinduism, a religion of umpteen gods, is the predominant religion of India, practised by the vast majority, nearly 80%, of its population and promoted mainly through numerous Hindu committees, which generally administer temples and other religious places and organize religious *melas* and other holy events. Practising Hindus normally worship many deities, fervently celebrate religious festivals and regularly perform numerous holy rites and rituals, which are, according to the Hindu folklore and priests with scriptural knowledge, essential to gratify Hindu gods so that they bless the devotees with their prayers. But the question is, how can the increasingly extravagant practices followed in the name of one god or another be overlooked, rationalized or justified, especially in view of the fact that we, the mere earthly mortals, have scarcity as an integral part of our natural destiny?

## RELIGION AND MY FAMILY

Having grown up in the lap of a pious Meitei[1] Hindu couple, who practiced both Sanamahism[2] and Hinduism and would, on rising from the bed, never put their feet on the earth floor without first paying their daily homage to Earth Mother by performing the Meitei customary practice of *laibak katpa*[3], I am familiar enough with the typical religious practices of a Meitei Hindu household. Indeed, religion has always been an integral part of my family's existence, though let me declare myself to be a human being who is a diehard believer in the goodness of believing in a righteous god or gods but does not subscribe to any of the extravagant practices of religion. Actually, at the risk of sounding blasphemous, let me also admit to being someone who thinks that religion and the idea of god(s) are mutually exclusive.

---

1. Meiteis are an indigenous community of Manipur, formerly known as Kangleipak, with its chronology being traceable as far back as 33 AD, when the reign of Nongda Lairen Pakhangba began. Major Meitei settlements are also found in two other states, Assam and Tripura and in two neighbouring countries, viz. Bangladesh and Myanmar.

2. Sanamahism is the original religion of Meiteis, and primarily involves the daily worship of Ema Leimarel Sidabi and Her son Lainingthou Sanamahi, the two main deities among the Meitei pantheon. As it is basically supposed to be compatible with Hinduism, except the latter's castiest part, and also because of historical compulsions, most if not all Meitei households today practise both the religions with equal fervour.

3. The Meitei customary practice of *laibak katpa* is done by first touching any given object of veneration with the fingertips of usually the right hand and then instantly withdrawing and touching the forehead with those fingertips, often three times. It is also a Meitei way of expressing regret for touching an object of veneration, say a holy object or a book, or an older person with one's foot by mistake.

My family's daily religious routine begins with the morning worship of the *tulsi* with smouldering incense sticks and ends with the dusk worship of Ema Leimarel Sidabi and Lainingthou Sanamahi also with smouldering incense sticks. While my beloved parents were alive, it was also one of their daily religious rituals to put a morsel of food beside their respective plates as their offering to deities before proceeding to actually eat their meal. As I used to eat in the same plate with my beloved father, I sometimes played the deities' part by swiftly picking up and eating the morsel at the end, usually followed by my father's light slap in the back of my head. I can now estimate that if those morsels of food had been saved in their raw form, at least 15 kg of rice and 11 kg of vegetables would have been saved every year, not to mention mustard oil, salt, chilli and other seasonings. Though I do not question the positive effect of being pious, I cannot but totally disagree with any religious practice that causes any waste of food, however little, a morsel, a mouthful or a handful.

Despite being low on the socio-economic scale, my family observes with great fervour most religious festivals and rituals, be it *Lamta Thangja*[4], Emoinu *Eratpa*[5], Durga Puja or Diwali, sparing no expense to ensure that all their ritualistic requirements are fully met. This is true of most Meitei Hindu households, poor and rich. Moreover, it is a common practice among Meitei Hindu families to turn to local priests whenever a serious trouble arises, say a family member falling seriously ill or meeting with an accident. When consulted, a priest may be expected to trot out the same old explanations of Shani, Rahu, Ketu, etc. and recommend a holy puja and/or an amulet or amulets. Such a puja is usually performed at his/her temple if he/she owns or manages one and also a costly

---

4. The *Lamta Thangja* rituals are performed among Meitei households in *Lamta*, the last month of the Meitei calender, with the aim of warding off evil spirits.
5. The Meitei festival of worshipping Goddess Emoinu and seeking Her blessings for a generally productive and prosperous year.

affair, involving a sacrifice or offering as a holy means of escaping from the clutches of evil forces or pacifying an angry deity.

According to my elder brother, who is currently the only earning member in our family, the total annual expenditure of our family on day-today religious activities and observance of religious festivals is about ₹ 5,300. He also confided to me that just a few weeks before, he had taken his *kuthi (kundli)* to a local priest-cum-astrologer at the 'combined' insistence of his wife and mother-in-law because he had developed an apparently serious health problem or, more precisely, some pulmonary infection. He said that though he had already started consulting a pulmonary specialist, his wife and mother-in-law had brought a lot of pressure to bear on him to urgently get his *kuthi* 'studied' by a renowned priest so as to find a divine remedy for his health problem. So reinforcing his reputation of being a worthy and obedient husband and son-in-law, he had happily obliged them.

Studying my brother's *kuthi,* the priest-cum-astrologer effectively convinced him to have a Shanidev pacification puja performed, in connection with which he had to buy about ₹500's worth of puja items like incense sticks candles, oil, earthen pot and plates and an assortment of fruits. At the end of Shanidev pacification puja, my brother handed over an amount of ₹333 (a holy figure quoted by the priest-cum-astrologer) to him as *dakhina* (Manipuri term for officiating fee), without paying which a puja will be treated in the nature of *tamas,* vide Verse 13, Chapter 17 (The Threefold Division of Faith) of the Bhagavad Gita. Also, of some interest is the fact that the priest-cum-astrologer returned only a small portion of whatever eatable offered to Shanidev as *prasad* to my brother and kept the rest for himself and, of course, other members of his family too. If the total cost of such irregular pujas is also added to the estimated annual expenditure on routine religious activities, not to mention the *opportunity cost* of time and energy wasted, then the annual expenditure estimate vis-à-vis my household's religious activities will swing upwards by a significant amount.

When I asked my brother what he felt about having to shell out over ₹5,300 per year for religious activities, from which he would never get any tangible results, except some brief solace and, perhaps, a fleeting sense of satisfaction of being able to normally keep up with the religious norms of society, and, of course, to do what his wife and mother-in-law said was important, he replied rather curtly, 'You can't afford to spare any expense where deities are concerned.' That reply effectively precluded me from proceeding with my plan to discuss a little about the obvious wastefulness of our family's disproportionate expenditure on religious activities. Because he would easily misunderstand me as trying to indirectly reason with him to forgo certain religious activities and divert the amount to be saved thus to his two sons' education or something like that, which will, however, be a change for the better, at least from my perspective.

## THE INFORMAL QUESTIONNAIRE SURVEY

During the third quarter of 2019, I had an Informal Questionnaire Survey (IQS) of eleven Meitei Hindu households, including my own, conducted vis-à-vis their annual expenditure on religious activities. But for my being in prison, I would have covered a wider sample of households randomly chosen in a statistically appropriate manner. However, I had to limit the IQS to only those eleven households, which were selected simply on the basis of my personal perception that they would be most forthcoming about what I needed to know for this paper.

I came to learn from the IQS that all the eleven households surveyed spend thousands of rupees on religious activities every year. A comparative analysis of the eleven households in terms of their annual income and expenditure on religious activities reveals that a household with a higher income level follows a broader range of religious activities and, therefore, spends more money on them than a lower income counterpart. But the higher the level of income, the lower the percentage of income spent on religious activities.

Let me share some relevant pieces of data gathered through the IQS. Beginning with those of my own household, which is at the bottom in terms of annual income among the eleven households surveyed, the estimated annual expenditure of my household on religious activities is about ₹5,300. This is 4.91% of my household's estimated annual income of ₹1.08 lakhs. Then my maternal aunt's household, also covered by the IQS and having the median annual income estimate among the eleven households, spends about ₹11,000 every year on religious activities, which is approximately 2.69% of its estimated annual income of ₹4.10 lakhs. So it is now clear that though the estimated annual expenditure of my maternal aunt's household on religious activities is higher than that of my household, it spends a smaller percentage (2.69%) of its estimated annual income than my household, which correspondingly spends 4.91%.

Indeed, the higher annual expenditure of my maternal aunt's household on religious activities is primarily on account of its observance of a wider range of religious activities than my family. Apart from all those religious festivals and rituals that my household observes, my maternal aunt's additionally observes *Vishwakarma Puja, Govardhan Puja,* etc. and conducts some special religious ritual on every *Purnima* (full moon), though both the households follow a similar routine of day-to-day religious activities. Moreover, it is a daily practice of my maternal aunt, a fish vendor, to offer at least ₹5, usually in the form of a coin, to Ema Keithel Lairembi (the Goddess of the bazaar) as a way of seeking Her blessings and also thanking Her for sustaining the bazaar.

Among those eleven households surveyed, my friend Bemma's enjoys the highest annual income of about ₹24 lakhs and normally spends about ₹26,000 per annum, or approximately 1.08% thereof on religious activities. The estimated annual expenditure of

Bemma's household on religious activities is more than double the corresponding figure of my maternal aunt's and nearly five times that of my own. As noted earlier, the gap between my maternal aunt's household and mine in terms of the estimated annual expenditure on religious activities is primarily due to the former's observance of a higher number of religious festivals and rituals than my household. But what causes Bemma's family to shell out for its religious activities more than double the corresponding figure of my maternal aunt's household is the bigger scale on which the former organises all its religious activities. For example, my maternal aunt's household celebrates Diwali modestly at an estimated cost of ₹1,500 only, offering an assortment of fruits, some flowers and stuff to Goddess Lakshmi and also with a few candles lit outside the house; whereas Bemma's household does it in a grand fashion, spending more than ₹5,000 on decorating the house with strings of flowers and coloured lights, distributing confectionary to dear and near ones, worshipping Goddess Lakshmi with highly elaborate arrangements and so on.

Indeed, all the eleven households or most of their members believe that their religious activities are a necessity for the sake of gratifying their deities and therefore absolutely sacrosanct. So they cannot even think of sparing any expense to elaborately carry out their religious activities.

It is also a common practice among Meitei Hindus to wear amulets, charms and stones fixed in rings and lockets for a wide variety of beliefs such as keeping evil forces at bay and drawing cosmic energy. Indeed, out of the fifty-nine members of the eleven households surveyed, forty-six are reported to wear a total of 161 amulets and charms, or an average of 3.5, with each costing anywhere between ₹300 and ₹2,500. According to one of the surveyed households, a set of 3 bronze amulets stuffed with some 'holy' material was procured from a renowned local priest-cum-astrologer at a huge cost of ₹4,500, exclusive of his consultation fees. Ironically, the person wearing the amulets, whose intrinsic value may be ₹30 a piece at most, is the most educated member of the household and a government employee too. Even children as young as 5 years are also reported to wear amulets and charms. Moreover, seventeen adult members of the eleven households wear twenty-seven protective stones in their rings and lockets, with the reported costs of those stones adding up to ₹74,000.

Now the big question is, have they been blessed with what they have been worshipping the deities of their faith for? Or have they become immune to the problems of life by virtue of their costly religious activities or the amulets, charms and stones, for that matter? Their answers lie in the fact that each of the eleven households today remains confronted with one or more of the common socio-economic and personal challenges like unemployment, alcohol addiction, husband-wife quarrel, sibling discord and the only son leaving his own ageing parents for his in-laws. Also, each of them has at least one member with a persistent medical problem like diabetes and high blood pressure.

Apart from some transient positive vibes that usually flow from religious activities such as daily worship and observance of a holy festival, the practice of Hinduism or any other religion, for that matter, cannot be presumed to attain anything divine but humanly perceptible or verifiable, though one may still take recourse to the Vedantic theory of Maya in Hinduism as an explanation thereof, or even subjectively argue that one can actually be worse off without one's religious activities. So why don't our religious activities, performed at considerable cost to our time and money, deliver what they are supposed to? There are two possible but mutually exclusive answers to this question:

1. The deities we worship do exist but are definitely not pleased with our mostly if not entirely extravagant way of worshipping them. For example, we waste lakhs of litres of milk every year, especially in washing the *lingam*, when millions of our children remain malnourished because of their under-consumption of nutritious diet. So our benevolent deities simply choose to remain passive and leave us to bear the consequences of our religious extravagance. Or;

2. The deities are nothing but fictitious characters around which legends and values were invented by some extraordinary minds with the dual idea of influencing the general conduct of people in a direction deemed desirable as per their own philosophies, and perhaps interests too, and seeking their unconditional obeisance by striking some fear of the unknown into their heart and mind or under pain of divine retribution.

Whichever of the two answers or whatever else may be the right answer, what is called for is a paradigm shift in terms of how deities are worshipped and their blessings sought.

## THE CONCEPT OF ECONOMICAL PIETY

As far as the idea of God/gods is concerned, it is fundamentally associated with the universe of morality, which is basically meant to guide man towards a pious life. So, also considering the common perception among believers that gods are eternally in favour of righteousness and, by the same token, eternally against what is not righteous, it should not be difficult at all for those believers in a sound state of mind to find the high road to the holy heart by doing some serious introspection and taking a deep submersion in the water of what I call **economical piety**; and 'economical' is the operative word of the phrase.

Based on the simple logic or belief that a benevolent and righteous god should and will never demand or accept anything wasteful, be it an extravagant holy ritual, ceremony or practice, whether or not prescribed in the Hindu/divine scriptures, mostly written thousands of years ago, and further on the conditional logic that if any god does, it cannot be considered benevolent or righteous or even worthy of worship, my concept of economical piety underlines that the devotees of a benevolent and righteous god are naturally supposed to desist from indulging in any extravagant practices in the name of worshipping it, the primary reason being that doing anything extravagant as part of the worship effectively runs counter to its very purpose. To bear this out, let me cite the hypothetical case of two devotees, x and y, of Goddess Saraswati, the Devi of knowledge. On the holy day of Saraswati Puja, x performs an elaborate worship of Goddess Saraswati from 06:00 am to 06:30 am, lighting up some incense sticks, kneeling or sitting in front of Her picture and reciting Her mantra throughout; whereas y, during the same period, just closes his eyes, pictures the resplendent image of Goddess Saraswati for a couple of seconds, recites Her name for a minute and then manages to memorize a few English words and digest a few general and academic snippets in the name of the Devi of knowledge. So by 06:31 am y's English vocabulary and general and academic knowledge get expanded by the few words and snippets he has just assimilated than x's, ceteris paribus (other things being equal). This means that Goddess Saraswati, assuming Her absolute control over knowledge, is more pleased with y's simple yet frugal style of worshipping Her than the lengthy one of x and has, therefore, rewarded y with greater knowledge than x, who could have used his valuable resources --- money spent on incense sticks and time --- in a more meaningful and productive manner.

## REVISITING THE HOUSEHOLDS SURVEYED

Picking up on the eleven households, it may now be argued that most if not all of their religious activities are obviously not in line with the concept of economical piety. In other words, their religious activities are mostly extravagant and apparently serve no other purposes than conforming to the traditional modalities of religion. Let me present but three examples:

Example 1: Bemma's household spends at least ₹5,000 on celebrating Diwali, the festival of lights, on which Goddess Lakshmi is also worshipped. Out of that amount, about ₹3,500 is spent only on multi-coloured electric lighting arrangements, which are draped around the house and usually left for many days after Diwali, thereby incurring an extra electricity charge, not to mention the environmental cost of generating electricity. Because of the absence of any young male member, Bemma's household has to forgo fireworks, another common feature of Diwali, which would otherwise push up its total expenditure on the festival. But the question is, how can the extravagant celebration of Diwali, which also involves the worship of the goddess of wealth, gratify Her or be rationalized or justified at all?

By the time the celebration of Diwali gets over, Bemma's household gets poorer by the amount of money spent on its wasteful items, plus whatever extra electricity charge incurred on account of the unnecessary multi-coloured lighting arrangements, thus indicating a negative reward from Goddess Lakshmi because of the extravagant manner in which it celebrates Diwali. Instead of wasting ₹3,500 — an amount enough for a poor average-size household to live through 20 days in rural India — on the lighting arrangements of Diwali, if Bemma's household saves the amount, it remains available for spending on other meaningful purposes, say getting the electric fittings of the house regularly checked by a handyman and buying a blanket or a jacket for a homeless person in the winter. This availability of ₹3,500 may be construed as a positive reward from Goddess Lakshmi.

Now, assuming a uniform annual spending of ₹3,500 on purposeless Diwali lights, if Bemma's household looks back only on the last ten years, the cumulative total expenditure on those Diwali lights works out at ₹35,000. So it may be said that over the last ten years, Bemma's household has become worse off by more than ₹35,000, only on account of purposeless Diwali lights, including whatever interest that could have been earned cumulatively over the period. The longer the look-back period, the higher the cumulative amount of money wasted on Diwali lights.

But then, one may argue, macrocosmically though, that if the bottom falls out of a particular commodity, say multi-coloured lights, compulsory redundancy of workers employed to produce such lights arises, leading to a rise in unemployment rate, drawdown on the savings of workers made redundant, greater pressure on social security schemes and so on. But a systematic diversion of capital from the production of multi-coloured lights for Diwali into other purposeful economic activities will certainly offset the overall negative effects arising from the sudden death of demand for multi-coloured lights.

As for the money to be squandered by households on multi-coloured Diwali lights, mostly imported from China, if it is somehow passed on to our poor maids, drivers, cleaners, vegetable vendors and the like by way of bonuses, perks and even tips, spent on sensible things or else saved, the aggregate demand especially by people of those descriptions for essential goods and services in particular will get a big boost, thereby not only generating more jobs in relevant industries and giving a boost to production but also lowering pressure on social security schemes like the MGNREGA and PMGRY, and helping narrow socio-economic disparities. And what else can be a better way of worshipping Goddess Lakshmi than boosting the income of the socio-economically less fortunate ones by forgoing Diwali lights and other purposeless items? If our celebrating Diwali less brightly and colourfully, without any of those multi-coloured lights, can bring greater 'socio-economic light' to the lives of the underprivileged, it is important that we do it; and maybe it is also what Goddess Lakshmi wants us to do.

Alternatively, if the money is saved, the country's savings rate will, theoretically speaking, get some boost, which will, in turn, lead to higher investment and then to a rise in employment rate, higher demand for consumption of goods and services, higher growth in tax revenue and so on. All of these imply an economic virtuous circle, which will lead to a better state of the economy and nation. So it can now be concluded that Goddess Lakshmi favours and rewards the forgoing of Diwali lights and other purposeless items for humanitarian and socio-economically more sensible considerations.

But what if Bemma's household asks, "How does it matter to others if we spend or squander our money on decorating our house with multi-coloured lights or on conforming to socio-cultural norms?" This is not a question but an unambiguous admission of hypocrisy and of impiety for Lakshmi, the Devi of wealth, exacting which is one of the purposes of this paper.

Example 2: This is on one of the eleven households that has an alcoholic member who drinks *yoo* (locally distilled Manipuri liquor) day and night and spends more than half of his daily wage on it. Swayed by what some superstitious people say about her husband's addiction to *yoo*, including her own close relatives, the alcoholic's wife has apparently come to believe that her husband has got addicted to *yoo* because of some *potsem jadu* (black magic) done to him by his ill-wisher(s). So she admits to having consulted three renowned local priests for an effective divine solution to her husband's allegedly black magic-driven addiction to *yoo*. On their advice, three special pujas are said to have been performed in succession over a period of 10 months with the aim and hope of having the *potsem jadu* removed from her husband's being.

Moreover, she has already had five amulets made for her husband with a view to providing him with a holy shield against evil effects and forces. According to her own calculation, she has spent a total of about ₹17,000 on trying to pull her husband through his deteriorating addiction to *yoo* by holy means like pujas and amulets, but to no avail. What is more, her husband's addiction has been complicated by the fact that he has recently developed alcohol-related health issues, both physical and mental, such as loss of appetite, abnormal liver function as indicated by his LFT reports, increasing irritability and aggressiveness, etc.

Indeed, hers is clearly a classic case of barking up the wrong tree under the potent influence of socio-culturally transmitted superstitious beliefs and social misguidance too. Had she taken her alcoholic husband to a proper rehab centre rather than turning to those deceitful *soi-disant* priests and bought him some detoxification medicine instead of having those five amulets made, her husband's addiction to *yoo* would already have gone or, at least, been mitigated significantly.

The misguided wife also admits that in her every worship since her husband's addiction to *yoo* came to her knowledge, her primary prayer has been his complete recovery from it, which has not been answered yet. This also implies that the deities she worships are, perhaps, not pleased with her approach to her husband's addiction, or the way she worships them. Or maybe they simply do not exist! Whichever be the actual case, what is immediately needed is a change of tack on her part, which means forgetting what the *soi-disant* priests say, forgetting the *potsem jadu* theory, disabusing herself of the presumed power of the amulets and, above all, rushing him to an accredited rehab clinic as soon as possible and strictly following whatever scientific advice it gives. This is most probably what the benevolent deities actually want done, if they exist at all!

Example 3: The third and last example is all about incense sticks, *dhoop*, candles, cotton/fibre wicks for lamps and *diyas*, oil, match-sticks, etc., which are essential for most if not all religious activities of Hindu households and temples. But let me raise a few questions here. Assuming gods to be benevolent, righteous and sensible, why would they prefer to be worshipped in a smoky, unhealthy environment, with all those carbon-emitting items smouldering and/or burning right under their nose? Again, why would they require their devotees to squander their hard-earned money on those unnecessary items, whose production and consumption pollute the environment? If it is all about putting their piety to the test, why didn't gods prescribe in the scriptures some mentally and physically more challenging but carbon-neutral, clean and healthy modes of worship, say, a 10-minute jogging in the park, a 1-km uphill walk or a 20-minute voluntary neighbourhood cleaning session, with prayers on the lips, which would not only help them stay fit, but also save a considerable amount of money and are environment-friendly too? These questions are, of course, humanly impossible to answer unless, of course, one is pretty familiar with invoking the Vedantic theory of Maya, which has been the ultimate refuge for whatever in Hinduism flies in the face of reason.

It may, of course, be a time-honoured practice of Hinduism to use carbon-emitting items such as incense sticks, *dhoop*, candles, oil lamps and *diyas* for worshipping deities. However, gods or no gods, change, being the only constant, is always desirable if it is for the better like the eradication of the inhumane, uncivilized practice of *Sati* and diminution of casteism.

In actual fact, there is no reason whatsoever to believe that gods are happier or more responsive if worshipped with incense sticks, *dhoop*, candles, oil lamps and *diyas*, and other carbon-emitting items. If and when we, Hindus, cease to use them in our religious activities, we will certainly be better off by the amount of money that would otherwise be spent on them, not to mention the time and energy to be saved and overall pollution to be avoided. And, this may be construed as an example of divine blessing in answer to a change for the better.

As far as the eleven Meitei Hindu households are concerned, they also spend an average of ₹3,600 per annum on those items for religious purposes only. This is definitely no small amount and will certainly stand them in good stead if saved or invested wisely. For example, ₹3,600 enough to take out an annual health insurance policy, which can safeguard a household against medical uncertainties for a year. It can also buy over 100 kg of good-quality rice from a regular grocery or four subsidized domestic LPG bottles, plus 250 kg of rice under the National Food Security Act, 2013. Indeed, there are umpteen other ways of spending the amount beneficially rather than on carbon-emitting items for religious purposes. But do we have the courage of our convictions to break free from our religious norms?

## A MACRO-ANALYSIS OF THE EXTRAVAGANT PRACTICES OF HINDUISM

Hinduism is practised by over a billion people worldwide, with the vast majority being Indians. Though it is a religion of a multitude of gods, the Hindu trinity of Lords Brahma, Vishnu and Shiva is considered its ultimate base. With lakhs of temples operating around Hinduism and crores of households strictly following it and its rituals, a massive quantity of incense and match-sticks, millions of cotton and fibre wicks, tonnes of *dhoop* and thousands of litres of oil get reduced to smoke, soot and ashes daily in running those temples and performing Hindu rituals at household level. It is true that I do not have any statistically generated estimate of the daily or yearly cost of using those carbon-emitting items in temples and homes. But it is just obvious that the actual cost thereof has to run into a few crores of rupees every day and thousands every year, which is more than enough to properly feed the entire homeless population of India.

Furthermore, millions of litres of milk are wasted every year in following some Hindu rituals, especially the milk-bathing of the *linga* and other idols. Thousands of tonnes of fresh fruits are also left to rot in the plates of Hindu temples and households every year in the name of deities. If we as a nation had the sense to ensure that the milk and fruits thus wasted actually reached the underfed stomach of millions of our undernourished and hungry fellow Indians, our gods would certainly have blessed us with the state of a stronger and healthier nation, making it possible to take pride in our Indianhood a fortiori.

What is no less outrageous is the increasingly extravagant style of showcasing religiosity, as witnessed by the rising expenditure on religious festivals, rites and rituals. For example, the Santosh Mitra Square Committee (Kolkata) used a ₹40-crore silver chariot reportedly sponsored by a jewellery brand, to ferry the idol of Goddess Durga during the 2019 celebration of Durga Puja. In the previous year, the same committee had also adorned the idol of Goddess Durga with a sari made of 30 kg of gold worth over ₹9 crore even then. But assuming a motherly nature of Goddess Durga on the basis of Her femininity, wouldn't She have been more gratified if the committee in question and its sponsors had shown the guts and humanitarian resolve to raise as much money as the monetary value of either the gold sari or the silver chariot, which they were bragging about, towards bringing hundreds of poor households of Kolkata out of poverty or build a massive housing complex to house some of the City of Joy's homeless and joyless people in Her name?

According to the 2011 Census, India then had a total of 2.1 million schools and colleges, whereas the number of places of worship stood at 3.1 million, occupying lakhs of hectares of prime land. Indeed, this is an enough area for building up millions of dwelling units, plus thousands of schools, colleges, research institutes and hospitals, which are desperately needed in this country. If the prime parcels occupied and other assets owned by religious bodies in India were to be monetized, they would conveniently fetch trillions of rupees, which may well be sufficient to free every poor Indian household from the prison of poverty.

Moving on to the liquid wealth of our temples, it is no secret that they are in possession of gold and silver worth trillions of rupees and also receive thousands of crores in donations every year. The famous Padmanabhaswamy Temple in Kerala alone is reported to own gold worth over ₹2 trillion at today's rate. The Tirumala Tirupati Venkateshwara Temple in Andhra Pradesh, considered the second wealthiest temple in India, is also reported to receive about ₹650 crore per annum in donations and make over ₹75 crore per annum only by selling *laddus*. These are but two examples of how wealthy our temples actually are! There are also many other Indian temples commanding liquid wealth estimated at thousands of crore rupees each.

But it is a matter of great concern that when our temples keep on hoarding wealth, their massive surplus wealth is just left to lie idle or used to create more wealth of their own. This seems like a sadistic indifference to the perennial shortage of funds confronting the nation on the socio-economic development front, especially for anti-poverty programmes, which can, of course, be financially turbocharged by channelling the surplus wealth of our temples into them. Indeed, our benevolent and righteous gods should be by far more pleased if the humongous surplus wealth of our temples is actually used to improve the deplorable conditions of crores of Indians who are helplessly languishing in abject poverty, with a large section of them living below the subsistence level.

Coming back to the extravagant, unhealthy and polluting practice of using carbon-emitting items in our religious activities, if the 20-crore-plus Hindu households of India come to abandon or scale it down significantly, that will save us thousands of crore rupees every year; the surroundings of our homes and temples will be a lot cleaner; lakhs of trees and bamboos will be saved every year; and our carbon footprint will also drop significantly.

Also, if we, Hindus, abandon the habit of 'monopolizing' the deities with our lengthy praying sessions by cutting on our praying time and start diverting the amount of time thus saved to positive social, physical, economic and educational activities such as having a longer friendly exchange with our neighbours, doing a 30-minute workout with the name of our most beloved god on our lips, completing an extra piece of work in the name of Goddess Lakshmi and studying one more chapter in the name of Goddess Saraswati, we will all become socially more compatible, physically and mentally stronger and healthier, economically more productive and educationally more successful!

Last but not least, if we start planting a tree each on every major religious festival like *Janmashtami* and *Emoinu Eratpa* and perform some social service like voluntarily sweeping our streets and pavements, cleaning the drains and river banks and weeding in our neighbourhood, all in the name of our deities, our country and, by extension, the world, will become greener by millions of trees every year and by far cleaner and healthier; and environmental degradation will also be progressively mitigated. Indeed, this revolutionary way of celebrating a religious festival can even become a model for other countries and religions to study and adopt; and it will also give our gods a sigh of relief and a great reason why they should begin to take pride in being our gods! Anyway, what else can be a more practical and better way of paying tribute to and worshipping the Holy Ganges and Brahmaputra than doing our bit in reversing their pollution and keeping them clean?

# Chapter Six

# THE DIGITAL ANTI-SPEEDING CODE ENFORCEMENT ECOSYSTEM AND A BRIEF ANALYSIS OF ITS ECONOMIC IMPACT

> "The global cost of road accidents in developing and emerging nations is at least $100 billion a year. This is more than twice the total aid received from all bilateral and multilateral sources."
>
> Dr. Adnan Hyder

When someone dear to us dies even of natural causes, it is quite natural for us to get overwhelmed by grief and a strong sense of loss. So imagine how traumatic it will actually be for anyone of us if an avoidable road accident kills someone who really matters to us!

On 13th September 2019, *The Times of India* carried a report on road accidents in India, citing some road accident statistics of the Ministry of Road Transport and Highways. One particularly shocking statistic highlighted therein was that 1,47,913 persons had been killed in road accidents in 2017, with speeding alone being responsible for 67% of all road fatalities and 73% of all the injured. Just think about the shattering blow that those preventable road accidents must have given the families and friends of the unfortunate victims, some of whom might have been the sole breadwinners of their respective families, only children of couples, promising doctors, teachers, upright policemen and so on. Taken together, the deaths, injuries and destruction of properties caused by road accidents represent a massive loss to the nation as a whole. So the big question is, how can road accidents be minimized if not brought down to nought?

The introduction of heavier penalties, including imprisonment in serious cases, and strict enforcement of the Motor Vehicles Act can, of course, bring down the number of road accidents. However, it is still possible to further reduce the incidence of road accidents by adopting existing and emerging technology. Indeed, we have to think beyond the conventional ways and means of checking violation of traffic rules such as deployment of traffic police personnel and installation of speed cameras and humps.

**The Digital Anti-Speeding Code Enforcement Ecosystem** (hereafter referred to as the 'DACE Ecosystem' as its shorthand) is a good example of how current and emerging technology can be ingeniously tapped to minimize road accidents.

## THE CONCEPTUAL FRAMEWORK OF THE DACE ECOSYSTEM

What actually triggered my initial conception of the DACE Ecosystem was the same report of *The Times Of India*, cited in the second paragraph above. The primary purpose of the DACE Ecosystem is to digitally enforce a special code against speeding, which is by far the biggest cause of road accidents in India. It is basically built on two conceptual systems in the form of the GPS-enabled **Smart Speeding Monitor-cum-Notifier (SSMN)** and **Central System for Real-time Action against Speeding (CSRAS),** though two external entities, viz. **Traffic Police (TP)** and **Penalty Receiving Bank (PRB)**, also play their ancillary roles in the DACE Ecosystem, whose schematic diagram is given in Appendix 1.

The DACE Ecosystem presumes a rule or law requiring that every motor vehicle has the SSMN system installed and gets incorporated into it by signing up and filling in on the SSMN App[£] an e-application for incorporation, which is automatically forwarded to the CSRAS for processing. Let me now enlarge on the SSMN and CSRAS:

### The SSMN System

The SSMN System may be conveniently broken down into two parts for ease of analysis—hardware and software. The former is basically made up of the following conceptual components:

1. **Integrated Milometer/Speedometer Reader (IMSR)**, which can read the motor vehicle's milometer and speedometer and feed the SSMN App with their readings second by second.

2. **Integrated Fog/Rain Sensor (IFRS),** which forms a supplementary add-on as it will enable the SSMN App to adjust the speed limit in case of fog or rain.

3. **Multiple Networks Access Subscriber Identification Module (MNASIM),** which is actually a SIM card but with the extra capability to switch automatically from one mobile network to another depending on which network currently offers stronger signals so as to ensure better connectivity.

4. A smartphone that has the SSMN App installed constitutes the core device of the SSMN system. But, of course, a

---

£ The SSMN App is the actual interface between the SSMN system and CSRAS. Once developed, it may be published on the Google Play Store and Apple App Store so that motor vehicle owners can download it conveniently.

dedicated SSMN core device can also be developed and used instead of a smartphone.

So these are the main hardware components of the SSMN system, with the core device to be properly linked with the IMSR and IFRS using a special bus or even via Bluetooth. As far as the MNASIM card is concerned, any data usage through it can be charged post-paid periodically, depending how much data is consumed from which network.

Moving on to the software part, the SSMN App represents its control unit, though both the IMSR and IFRS have their own enabling software elements. Indeed, the SSMN App is an integrated suite of two programs, viz. **Digital Speed Limit Map (DSLM),** which is the core enabling program, and **Automatic Data Processing Module (ADPM),** which is the core processing program. These two programs are expanded on in the following paragraphs.

1. The DSLM is a digitized map with speed limits set for all routes covered by it, and hinges on satnav, say GPS (a standard feature of today's smartphones), to constantly feed the ADPM with the speed limit of its current route location. Some technically important considerations around its conception are as follows:

    1.1. As the same speed limit cannot be imposed on all types of motor vehicles, the DSLM must be set with different speed limits for different types of motor vehicles for the same route. The possibility of one type of a vehicle, say a bus, falsely using the speed limit of another, say a car, can be eliminated by a one-off setting option for the actual type of motor vehicle in the process of filling in the e-application for incorporation into the DACE Ecosystem or even by developing motor vehicle type-specific DSLM versions.

    1.2. The DSLM must be periodically updated by taking into account the changing conditions of roads, construction of new roads and closure of old ones, if any.

1.3. For the sake of greater speed flexibility, the DSLM must also have the capability to automatically change the speed limit of any route to suit different traffic periods that a day can actually be divided into and changing weather conditions as well. For example, if the speed limit is set at, say, 50 kmph during a normal traffic period, the DSLM must automatically bring it down to, say, 30 kmph during the rush hour. Another example is, if the IFRS senses fog or rain and communicates it to the DSLM, it must automatically change the normal weather speed limit into the fog- or rain-adjusted one as the same speed limit cannot be allowed for all weather conditions.

1.4. The DSLM must also have a special feature in the form of the **Faster Ride Mode (FRM)**, which can be activated in case of emergency or hurry. The FRM enables an SSMN system-installed motor vehicle to travel up to, say, 20% faster than the speed limit without the risk of a **Speed Limit Breach (SLB)**. But the following conditions apply:

a. The FRM is available for a maximum of 10 hours a month;

b. It cannot be activated during the DSLM-defined rush hour or while the fog- or rain-adjusted speed limit is on; and,

c. Its use is progressively chargeable.

However, these conditions are not applicable to ambulances, fire brigade vehicles and other emergency service vehicles.

2. The Automatic Data Processing Module (ADPM) automatically processes every bit of data flowing from the IMSR and DSLM. When the SSMN system is turned on, its GPS instantly locates it on the DSLM, which, in turn, communicates the corresponding speed limit to the ADPM. GPS keeps on tracking it and, by implication, its carrying vehicle on the DSLM second by second. When it moves from one stretch of road to another with a different speed limit, the DSLM instantly updates the ADPM on the new speed limit. The IFRS, on the other hand, updates the DSLM at regular intervals on weather conditions so as to prompt it to adjust the speed limit in case of fog or rain.

Coming to the IMSR, it directly feeds the ADPM in real time with the changing readings of milometer and speedometer, which are successively processed against every coincident unit of speed limit data flowing from the DSLM second by second.

When there arises a Speed Limit Breach (SLB), i.e. the speedometer reading exceeding its coincident speed limit, the ADPM instantly initiates the **Speeding Data Capturing Process (SDCP)** in four steps of 'Detect Register, Record and Forward' in the same order. For example, while moving along a route with a DSLM-set speed limit of, say, 100 kmph for cars, if a SSMN system-installed car exceeds 100 kmph, the ADPM instantly detects the SLB (step one in an SDCP), following which the SLB detection alarm is automatically set off. If the driver manages to do a **Speed Limit Unbreach (SLU)**, i.e. bringing the car's speed down to the speed limit or below, within a time limit, say, 4.9 seconds of the detection of the SLB, the ADPM terminates the current SDCP. But if not, it automatically registers a Speeding Instance (SI) and starts recording the emerging speeding data exactly at the fifth second (steps two and three respectively). The

ADPM keeps on recording every bit of data flowing from the IMSR against every coincident bit of data being fed by the DSLM in the form of changing location coordinates and corresponding speed limit until the car does an SLU, whereupon the ADPM instantly forwards the speeding data, recorded until the SLU, to the CSRAS in the form of a Speeding Instance Data Set (SIDS), thus bringing the current SDCP to its end.

In case of an IMSR failure, the ADPM has automatic recourse to a special feature that may be called **'IMSR-Backup Function' (IMSR-BF).** In case the ADPM has not received the milometer and/or speedometer readings from the IMSR for five consecutive minutes for whatever reason, it automatically initiates an IMSR-BF with the following sequential steps:

2.1. Drawing upon the time-series GPS coordinates and corresponding speed limit(s) received from the DSLM in the last five minutes;

2.2 Processing all the drawn-upon (and emerging) data as per an algorithm determining if there has been an SI on the basis of GPS coordinates and timings at 1 km route intervals and corresponding speed limit(s); and,

2.3 Forwarding the SIDS to the CSRAS in case an SI is confirmed and its SIDS subsequently generated in a special format.

Let me cite an explanatory example. While moving along a route with a DSLM-set speed limit of 30 kmph for cars, if a car was located by GPS at location $X_2Y_4$ at 02:01 pm after it had been located at $X_1Y_3$ at 02.00, with the distance between $X_1Y_3$ and $X_2Y_4$ being 1km, then the car is confirmed through the IMSR-BF to have committed an SI. If the car is confirmed in the same way to have committed another SI in covering the next 1km, the ADPM combines the two consecutive SIs, with the combining process continuing until the car is confirmed to have done an SLU by covering any following 1km within the speed limit, or more precisely, by taking at least 2 minutes to cover the distance of 1Km.

But even if the car is confirmed to have taken 2 minutes to cover a distance of 1km along the 30 kmph route, it could still have committed speeding in between by covering a length of, say, 500m in 30 seconds and the next 500m in 90 seconds. So it is essential that the route gap for computation is set at the shortest possible according to the current geolocation technology.

It is also important to note that IMSR-BF requires that every bit of data generated by the DSLM has a minimum retention period of five minutes. But all outgoing and incoming data sets need to be retained in the core device until they are manually deleted at the owner's discretion.

However, an important question arises here: What if the SSMN system is sought to be bypassed, say, by turning off the core device or just deactivating the SSMN App? In order to deal with this contingency, the ADPM must be programmed to cross-check the milometer reading and GPS coordinates last received from the IMSR and DSLM respectively on the SSMN system or App being turned off against those first received on being turned on. If the ADPM detects a 'route location' difference of a defined length between the last-received milometer reading and GPS coordinate pair and the first-received ones, it confirms a Bypassing Instance (BI) and thereafter generates its Bypassing Instance Data Set (BIDS), which is instantly forwarded to the CSRAS.

So the conceptual SSMN system now stands demonstrated quite extensively with a schematic diagram of its environment presented in Appendix 2, followed by a basic input-output diagram of the DSLM in Appendix 3 and an integrated flow chart of the ADPM in Appendix 4. Once it is installed, an e-application for its incorporation into the DACE Ecosystem is to be filled in on the SSMN App and submitted to the CSRAS, which processes and accepts the e-application if found in order. The CSRAS then incorporates the SSMN system into the DACE Ecosystem under the details of the motor vehicle, creates its Individual Motor Vehicle Folder (IMVF) and generates an e-confirmation of its successful incorporation, which is instantly sent to the motor vehicle's owner.[+]

## THE CSRAS

Having presented the architecture of the SSMN system, let me elaborate on the functionality of the CSRAS, which is the linchpin of the DACE Ecosystem. The CSRAS can take the form of a powerful server or even an integrated system of servers, which must be capable of simultaneously processing all incoming data sets from thousands of SSMN systems. Indeed, it will be processing all incoming data sets from an SSMN system in Bypassing/Speeding File Processing Rounds[@] (B/SFPRs), which run through three stages, with Stage 1 being common to all B/SFRPs. The three stages are expanded on in the following paragraphs.

### Stage 1

The CSRAS executes this stage in three steps, which are as follows:

1.1: It receives $B/SIDS_1$ from a motor vehicle in its Individual Motor Vehicle Folder[1] ($IMVF^1$).

1.2: It then analyses $B/SIDS_1$ and fixes a penalty for the current B/SI on the basis of a penalty-fixing algorithm. As B/SIs can vary in terms of distance and duration, and also degree in the case of

---

[+] Through the SSMN App, cc registered email address, mobile number, etc.

[@] A Bypassing/Speeding File Processing Round is the processing of a file of one or more B/SIDS's until the resulting penalty is complied with.

speeding, the penalty-fixing algorithm must ensure that different penalties are set for different B/SIs. The longer the distance and duration (and the higher the degree of speeding), the heavier the penalty should be.

1.3: Lastly, it generates, and forwards to the $MV^1$ owner[+], an e-Ticket for Bypassing/Speeding Instance$_1$ (e-TB/SI$_1$), detailing the amount of penalty, online payments links, implications in case of failure to pay the penalty within a specified period, reason(s) for the imposition of the penalty[#] and so on.

**Stage 2**

This stage opens up with two 'Possible but Mutually Exclusive Cases (PbMECs), i.e. 2.1 and 2.2, stemming directly from Step 1.3 in Stage1.

2.1: This is the possible case of e-TB/SI$_1$ being complied with within the specified period, say, 10 days, of its service. But this also throws up two 'Possible but Mutually Exclusive Subcases (PbMESs) in the form of 2.1A and 2.1B:

2.1A: e-TB/SI$_1$ is complied with within 10 days from its service, with no new B/SIDS(s) received in $IMVF^1$ in the meantime. So 2.1A constitutes the end of the first possible B/SFPR.

2.1B: Another data set in the form of B/SIDS$_2$, is received in $IMVF^1$ even before e-TB/SI$_1$ is complied with. It is also processed in the same way as the first B/SIDS; and the pending e-TB/SI$_1$ is aggregated with e-TB/SI$_2$, resulting from B/SIDS$_2$, into what is called 'Aggregate e-Ticked for Multiple Bypassing/Speeding Instances$_1$ (Ae-TMB/SI$_1$). In case more B/SIDSs are received, they are also processed in the same way. However, Ae-TMB/SI$_1$ or n is complied with within the specified period from the service of

---

# A penalty can actually be a fine, cancellation of driving licence and/or motor vehicle registration or even a jail term. But the penalty in this paper only means a fine.

e-TB/SI$_1$, thus bringing the second possible B/SFPR to its end in 2.1B.

2.2: This is the other possible case, in which e-TB/SI$_1$ is not complied with within the specified period of 10 days from its service, thereby giving rise to another two PbMESs in the form of 2.2A and 2.2B.

2.2A: e-TB/SI$_1$ is not complied with within 10 days from its service, though the CSRAS receives no new B/SIDS(s) in IMVF[1] in the meanwhile. This directly leads to Stage 3.

2.2B: Even before e-TB/SI$_1$ is complied with, another data set, B/SIDS$_2$, is received in IMVF[1]. It is also processed in the same way as B/SIDS$_1$; and the pending e-TB/SI$_1$ is aggregated with e-TB/SI$_2$, generated on the basis of B/SIDS$_2$, into Ae-TMB/SI$_1$. In case of receipt of even more B/SIDSs in IMVF[1], the CSRAS will be processing them in the same way. However, Ae-TMB/SI$_{1\text{ or n}}$ is not complied with within the specified period, i.e. 10 days from the service of e-TB/SI$_1$. So this naturally leads to Stage 3.

## Stage 3

In this stage, the CSRAS first executes two tasks parallel: First, 3.1, generating and serving the MV[1] owner[+] with an e-directive for surrender of MV[1] for failing to comply with the pending e-TB/SI$_1$ or Ae-TMB/SI$_{1\text{ or n}}$, as the case may be, within 10 days from the service of e-TB/SI$_1$, along with an e-notification of imposition of what may be called **Escalating Non-Compliance Fine (ENCF)** in the nature of a daily chargeable compound interest on penalty; and, second, 3.2, generating, and forwarding to the TP, an e-order to confiscate MV[1] at the earliest opportunity, along with the current B/SFPR MV[1] Geolocation Code, which is meant to enable the TP to locate MV[1] through GPS. Then two new PbMECs arise in the form of 3.3 and 3.4.

3.3: This is the one of the PbMECs in which the pending e-TB/SI$_1$+ENCF or Ae-TMB/SI$_{1\text{ or n}}$ +ENCF is complied with before the TP can actually impound $MV^1$, giving rise to two PbMESs in the form of 3.3A and 3.3B:

3.3A: e-TB/$SI_1$+ENCF or Ae-TMB/$SI_{1 \text{ or } n}$ +ENCF is complied with before the TP can actually confiscate $MV^1$ with no new B/SIDS(s) received in $IMVF^1$ in the meanwhile. So the CSRAS generates, and forwards to the TP, an e-notification of cancellation of the e-order to confiscate $MV^1$, cc its owner+, thus bringing the third possible B/SFPR to its end in 3.3A.

3.3B: The CSRAS receives in $IMVF^1$ another data set or more in the form of $B/SIDS_{2 \text{ or } n}$ even before e-TMB/$SI_1$ +ENCF is complied with. It processes $B/SIDS_{2 \text{ or } n}$ in the same way, generating Ae-TMB/$SI_{2 \text{ or } n}$ +ENCF and forwarding it to the $MV^1$ owner+. But before the TP can actually impound $MV^1$, Ae-TMB/$SI_{1 \text{ or } n}$ +ENCF is complied with. So the CSRAS generates and forwards to the TP, an e-notification of cancellation of the e-order to confiscate $MV^1$, thus finishing the third possible B/SFPR in 3.3B.

3.4: In this last possible case, e-TB/$SI_1$+ENCF or Ae-TMB/$SI_{1 \text{ or } n}$+ENCF is not complied with before the TP ultimately confiscates $MV^1$. This inevitably gives rise to another two PbMESs in the form of 3.4A and 3.4B, which are enlarged upon as follows:

3.4A: As e-TMB/$SI_1$+ENCF or Ae-TMB/$SI_{1 \text{ or } n}$+ENCF is not complied with, the TP impounds $MV^1$, though the CSRAS does not receive any new B/SIDSs in the meantime.

3.4B: In this possible subcase, the CSRAS receives in $IMVF^1$ another data set or more in the form of $B/SIDS_{2 \text{ or } n}$ even before e-TMB/$SI_1$+ENCF or Ae-TMB/$SI_{1 \text{ or } n}$+ENCF is complied with. It also processes the new B/SIDS(s) in the same way, generating, and forwarding to the $MV^1$ owner+, AeTMB/$SI_{1 \text{ or } n}$ +ENCF.

In either of 3.4A and 3.4B, the TP actually confiscates $MV^1$ for failing to comply with e-TB/$SI_1$+ENCF or Ae-TMB/$SI_{1 \text{ or } n}$ + ENCF even after the service of the e-warning of its confiscation, along with the e-notification of ENCF. Once the pending e-TB/SI$_1$+ENCF or Ae-TMB/SI$_{1 \text{ or } n}$ +ENCF is complied with, the CSRAS generates, and forwards to the TP, an e-order to release MV$^1$ immediately, cc its owner+. As soon as the TP executes the e-order to release MV$^1$, it updates the CSRAS on the release of MV$^1$, instantly following which the latter generates, and sends to the MV$^1$ owner+, an e-notification of completion of the current B/SFPR.

To put the CSRAS in a nutshell, it forms the linchpin of the DACE Ecosystem, and operates in three stages, as elaborated above. To make its non-linear processing of B/SIDSs easier to grasp, a flow chart is given in two parts in Appendixes 6 and 7.

Moving on to the process of complying with an e-TB/SI or Ae-TMB/SI, with or without ENCF, it is basically a matter of paying the penalty specified therein. Indeed, it begins with the e-ticketed MV$^1$ owner paying the penalty through the SSMN App itself or any other acceptable mode of payment. On receipt of the penalty, the Penalty Receiving Bank (PRB) instantly generates, and forwards to the CSRAS, an e-confirmation of the receipt of the penalty, cc the MV$^1$ owner+. This can happen in either of the following two PbMECs.

1. The first possible case is that the CSRAS has yet to generate, and forward to the TP, the e-order to confiscate MV1 as the mandatory period within which to comply with e-TB/SI or Ae-TMB/SI has not elapsed yet. So on receipt of the e-confirmation of penalty deposit from the PRB, the CSRAS generates, and issues the MV$^1$ owner+ with, an e-acknowledgement of penalty compliance, along with an e-notification of the current B/SFPR's completion, thus bringing the current B/SFPR to its end.

2. The other of the two PbMECs is that the CSRAS has already generated, and forwarded to the TP, an e-order for immediate confiscation of MV$^1$, along with the current B/

SFPR MV$^1$ Geolocation Code. But this gives rise to two PbMESs, which are as follows:

2.1. The TP has yet to confiscate MV$^1$, whatever be the reason. So on receipt of the e-confirmation of penalty deposit from the PRB, the CSRAS instantly generates an e-notification cancelling the e-order to confiscate MV$^1$ and sends it to the TP. It also generates an e-acknowledgement of penalty compliance and sends it to the MV$^1$ owner$^+$, along with an e-notification of the completion of the current B/SFPR, thus bringing the current B/SFPR to its end.

2.2. The TP has already confiscated MV$^1$. So on receipt of the e-confirmation of penalty deposit from the PRB, the CSRAS generates, and issues the TP with, an e-order to release MV$^1$, cc its owner$^+$. Once MV$^1$ is released, the TP communicates the execution of the e-order to release MV$^1$ to the CSRAS, which, in turn, generates, and sends to the MV$^1$ owner$^+$, an e-notification of the completion the current B/SFPR, thus bringing the current B/SFPR to its end.

A flow chart of the non-linear process of complying with e-TB/SI or Ae-TMB/SI with or without ENCF and follow-through is presented in Appendix 8.

With the basic framework of the DACE Ecosystem broken down and explained, let me now attempt to address some potential issues about it. Making it mandatory by means of an amendment to the Motor Vehicles Act for MV owners to get the SSMN system installed and incorporated into the DACE Ecosystem may be interpreted as an imposition in terms of equipment and installation cost. Moreover, the restrictions that are bound to arise from getting incorporated into the DACE Ecosystem may, of course, be construed as a serious encroachment on civil liberties; and the provision for tracking a penalty-defaulting

MV down electronically is a threat to privacy. But the fundamental purpose of the DACE Ecosystem, that is to serve as an effective and formidable deterrent to speeding, unquestionably overrides those issues, which may, instead, be taken as a small price to pay for pre-empting the unavoidable and potential fallouts of speeding such as excessive consumption of fuel and tragic road accidents, not to mention the massive economic and personal loss unavoidably arising therefrom.

## NOVEL ADVANTAGES COMPARED TO OTHER SPEED ADAPTATION SYSTEMS IN EXISTENCE

Though there are other systems of controlling speeding primarily through mechanical intervention, generically known as 'Intelligent Speed Adaptation System,' the DACE Ecosystem has the following novel advantages to offer:

1. GPS-based real-time enforcement of an anti-speeding code.

2. Speed limit auto-adjustability algorithm, to be dictated not only by GPS coordinates, but also by other factors such as rain, fog, different periods of the day and/or any other relevant factor.

3. Instant updatibility of speed limits and other governing parameters.

4. No dependence on road signs or other roadside installations.

5. Universal applicability, meaning that every motor vehicle, be it a scooter, car or bus, old or new, can be brought under it.

6. Bypassing-proof logic.

7. Easy expandability of scope, meaning that other accident prevention functionalities like alcohol sensor, parking/

traffic light/one-way route violation detector, route diversion notification and accident alert systems can be incorporated into it.

8. Non-mechanical character.

## ENVISIONED PURPOSES

So what are the purposes that the DACE Ecosystem is envisioned to serve? They are as follows:

1. Watertight enforcement of an anti-speeding penal code in real time.

2. Formidable deterrence against speeding, which is by far the biggest cause of road accidents and casualties.

3. Effective prevention of speeding-driven accidents and, by implication, casualties.

4. Significant boost to road safety.

5. Cultivation of a public tendency towards safe driving/riding.

6. Minimization of the overall economic cost of speeding-driven accidents, to be reflected in:

    6.1. Reduction in speeding-induced wastage of fuel and also corresponding fall in carbon emissions.

    6.2. Avoidance of destruction of assets, particularly motor vehicles, in speeding-driven accidents.

    6.3. Potential fall in insurance premium rates vis-à-vis motor vehicles in the long run.

7. Last but most importantly, saving of lives and limbs through prevention of speeding-driven road accidents.

## THE DACE ECOSYSTEM'S ECONOMIC IMPACT

In her article *"The Road to Perdition,"* published in *The Economic Times*, Anjana Menon, CEO, Content Pixies, cites a 2016 study by the United Nations Economics and Social Commission for Asia and the Pacific (UNESCAP), which estimated that road accidents cause a 3% dent to the Indian economy. This is supported by a news item on the World Bank's report titled *"Delivering Road Safety in India,"* released at the *'Third Global Ministerial Conference on Road Safety'* in Stockholm, carried by *The Statesman* on 21$^{st}$ February 2020 under the headline *"India needs to invest $109bn to halve its crash fatalities in next decade: WB report."* It highlighted that road crashes impact economic growth, costing the Indian economy between 3 and 5% of the GDP. It is also stated therein that an estimated extra investment of $109 billion on India's road safety programmes over the next decade will bring economic benefits worth about 3.7% of the GDP. Though I have not studied either of the actual official reports of the UNESCAP's 2016 study and the World Bank's *"Delivering Road Safety in India,"* if their estimates vis-à-vis the impact of road accidents on the Indian economy are just taken for granted, it is absolutely easy to conclude that bringing the number of road accidents down to a minimum will certainly have a booster impact on the Indian economy.

It is true that the recent amendment to the Motor Vehicles Act was made with greater emphasis on checking accidents by means of enhanced penalties for violation of traffic rules and regulations. Now even driving/riding an uninsured motor vehicle can cost you nearly four times the pre-amendment penalty for the same. However, increasing the penalty is not going to be enough at all to deal effectively and satisfactorily with traffic rules violation and violators, especially when there exists no efficient enforcement environment.

It is no exaggeration to say that reckless drivers and riders do not bother much about the possible consequences of violating traffic rules as they are fully aware that the chances of getting caught are actually negligible. This is indeed a very big but low-visibility challenge. Moreover, it is very common and easy, as I have experienced first-hand, to go scot-free by bribing traffic police personnel on duty if ever caught breaking traffic rules. So it is little wonder that violation of traffic rules and road accidents continue unabated to India, with four separate accidents killing at least 35 people on the same day when the World Bank report in question was released, as was noted in the same news item of *The Statesman*.

However, it is such holes in the traffic law enforcement, especially concerning the speeding part, that the DACE Ecosystem can plug quite efficiently. Indeed, the DACE Ecosystem makes it literally impossible for speeding drivers and riders to evade getting caught and penalized, provided, of course, that the SSMN system is made temper-proof. So when drivers and riders become certain of getting caught and penalized for sure in case of speeding or any other traffic law violation on their part, they are least likely to do that.

As the vast majority of fatalities and injured causalities in road accidents, 67% and 73% respectively in 2017, had their actual cause in speeding, bringing speeding-prone drivers and riders to heel by means of the DACE Ecosystem or any other mechanism, for that matter, will certainly lead to the following succinctly defined results, inter alia:

1. A significant fall in the number of speeding instances and commensurate decline in speeding-related accidents and causalities, thus sparing thousands of families from the extreme trauma of loved ones sustaining injuries and losing their life.

2. An equivalent fall in the number of claims on life and motor vehicle insurance policies, which will enable insurance firms to bring down premium rates in due course, thereby significantly lightening the premium burden on the common people in the long run.

3. A drastic reduction in the general economic loss in the form of destruction of motor vehicles and other assets as well as wastage of human resources embodied in victims.

4. Effective prevention of unnecessary consumption of millions of litres of diesel and petrol through speeding every year, and also of resultant emission of tonnes of carbon dioxide into the atmosphere, thus bringing down the country's fuel consumption and carbon footprint and, by implication, the levels of pollution.

So those are some prominent potential effects of bringing the incidence of speeding down by virtue of the DACE Ecosystem or something else. It is true that apart from speeding there are many other causes of road accidents such as use of the mobile phone while driving/riding and drink-driving, which can, I am sure, also be addressed in a smart way through the adoption of modern technology. However, developing and introducing an all-encompassing system for smart enforcement of all traffic rules and regulations and bringing all motor vehicles under it will certainly be a highly complex and perhaps cost-prohibitive process, involving highly sophisticated devices and sensors and even application of artificial intelligence and machine learning. I have, therefore, consciously concentrated only on addressing the issue of speeding, which is by far the biggest cause of road fatalities and injured casualties in India.

According to my own calculations, based on current cost estimates, the development of the basic constituents of the DACE Ecosystem --- a prototype of the SSMN system, including its mobile app, and the CSRAS with a simultaneous processing capacity of one million B/SFPRs, along with the ancillary app for the TP --- can cost only about 7 crore INR, which is less than 1 million USD at the current exchange rate. But I admit to having presumed in my calculations the free availability of all the relevant data on roads and highways so that the development team does not have to go surveying them all just to collect the data required for setting appropriate speed limits in the DSLM.

As the cost of the SSMN system is meant to be borne by MV owners themselves, the DACE Ecosystem is not likely to spring any considerable extra cost, except the initial outlay on manpower raising, promotion and awareness campaign, construction of required structures and, of course, annual overheads, including the cost of periodically upgrading its physical components and updating its software components, especially the DSLM, which functions as the primary enabling program of the SSMN system.

So if the World Bank's report calls for an estimated extra investment of a whopping 109 billion USD over the next 10 years just to halve the country's road fatalities, then the DACE Ecosystem, with its minuscule estimated cost, is obviously the most cost-effective mechanism for managing the biggest cause of road accidents and casualties, that is speeding.

Now let me briefly discuss how voluntary incorporation into the DACE Ecosystem can be incentivized. Though making it mandatory for all motor vehicles to get the SSMN system installed and incorporated into the DACE Ecosystem and for the automotive industry to make all future motor vehicles DACE Ecosystem-compliant by making the SSMN system an integral part of their electronics will, of course, be an effective way of obliging them, taking recourse to legislation is not the only or best way of persuading people into something in a democratic polity like ours. So other more democratic ways and means must be explored. One such way is to educate MV owners on the potential long-term benefits of the DACE Ecosystem, though this will be a lengthy process. Another more attractive way is to offer a range of financial incentives in the form of road tax concessions, lower insurance premium rates, etc., which can greatly boost voluntary incorporation. For example, those MVs getting voluntarily incorporated within a certain period of time may be given a good discount off their toll tax. Also, those MVs that do not commit speeding in twelve consecutive months may be awarded significant insurance premium concessions. Such financial incentives will certainly be more visible and attractive to MV owners than any other benefit that the DACE Ecosystem can bring them and, by extension, the nation as a whole in the long run. As far as the revenue cost of giving out such financial incentives is concerned, the overall potential benefits to flow from the DACE Ecosystem outweigh it by far.

Lastly, if and when the DACE Ecosystem becomes a reality and starts acting as an effective brake on the deadly tendency towards speeding, we, the nation, can rest assured that Indian roads are now safer for us all to walk, ride and drive along!

# APPENDICES

**Appendix 1**
**Schematic Diagram of DACE Ecosystem**

DACE Ecosystem

- PRB
- SSMN System-installed Motor Vehicles
- CSRAS
- TP

# Appendix 2
## Schematic Diagram of SSMN System Environment

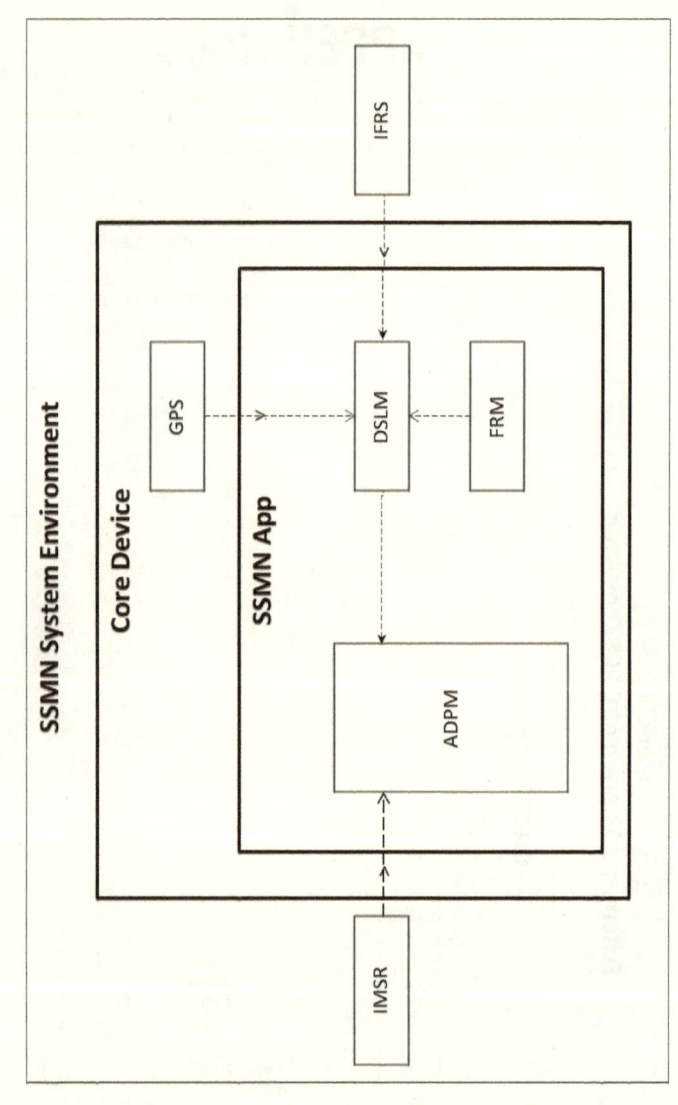

*Appendices* | **153**

# Appendix 3
## Basic Input-Output Diagram of DSLM

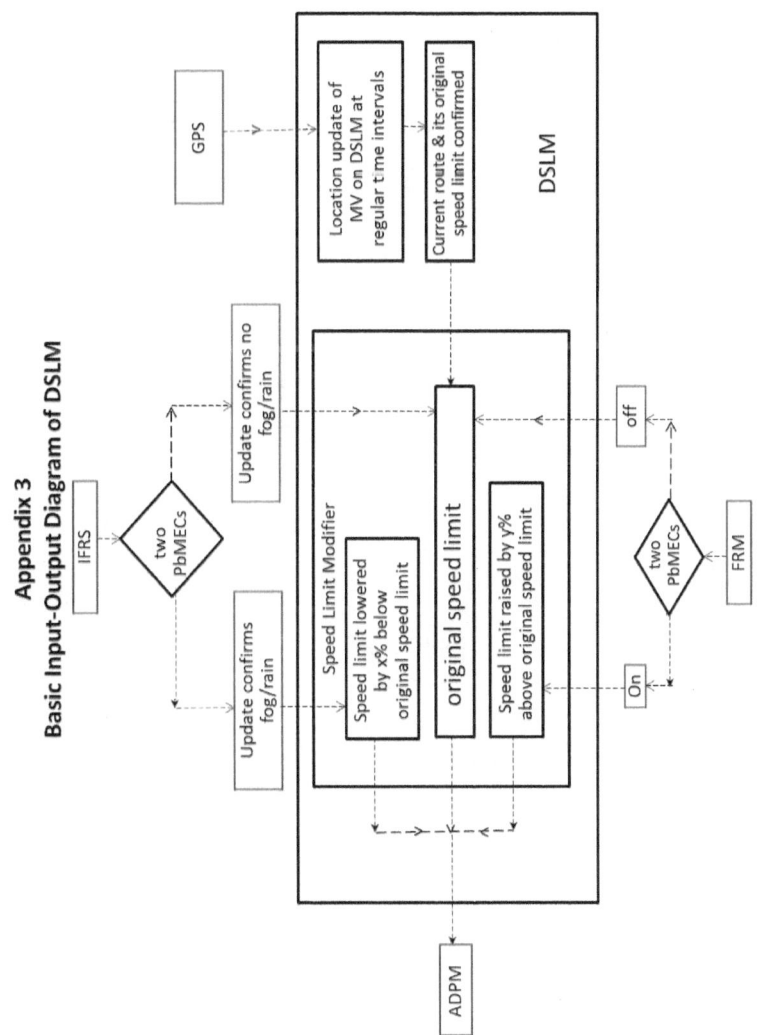

# Appendix 4
## Integrated Flow Chart of ADPM's Three Function Processes : BDCP, SDCP & IMSR-BF

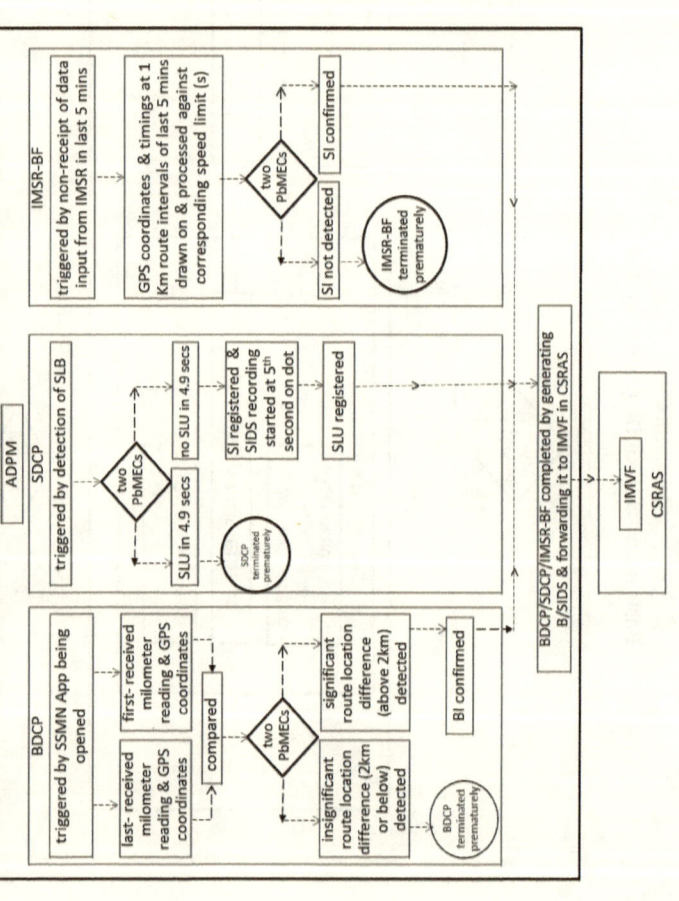

## Appendix 5
## Flow Chart of Incorporation of MV[1] into DACE Ecosystem

**MV[1]**
- SSMN System

**CSRAS**
- E-application for incorporation into DACE Ecosystem, containing all basic details of MV[1] such as owner's name, address & contact details, chassis & engine numbers, etc. filled in & forwarded to CSRAS
- e-application accepted on being found in order
- MV[1] Incorporated into DACE Ecosystem
- Individual Motor Vehicle Folder (IMVF[1]) created

- e-confirmation of incorporation into DACE Ecosystem generated & forwarded to MV[1] owner

**Appendix 6**
**Flow Chart of Non-Linear Processing of B/SIDS(s)**
**PART-I**

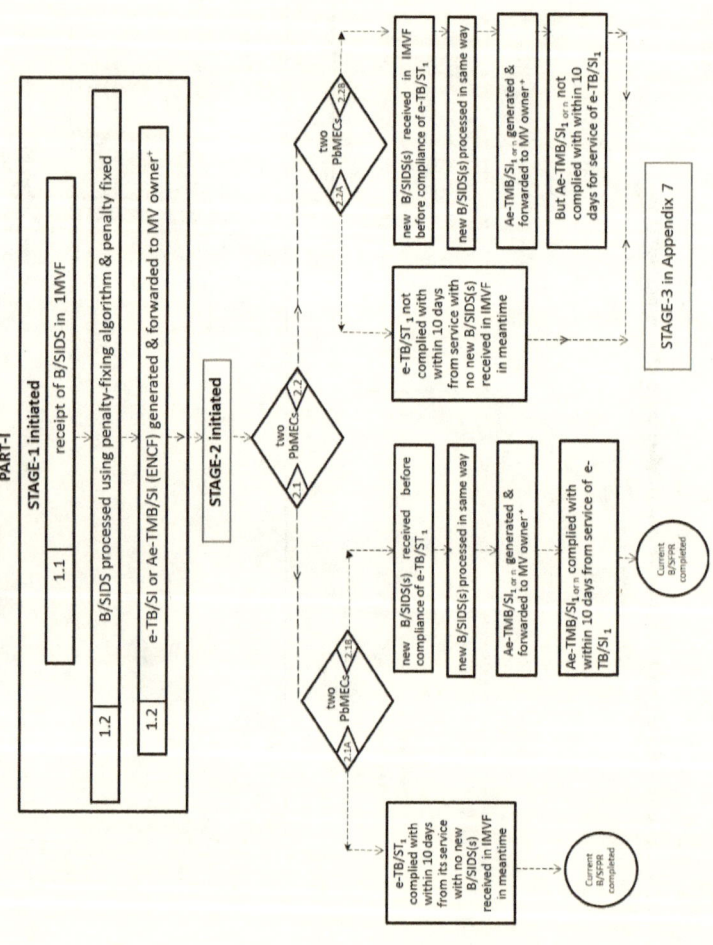

## Appendix 7
## Flow Chart of Non-Linear Processing of B/SIDS(s)
### PART-II

**STAGE-3 initiated with parallel execution of 2 tasks**

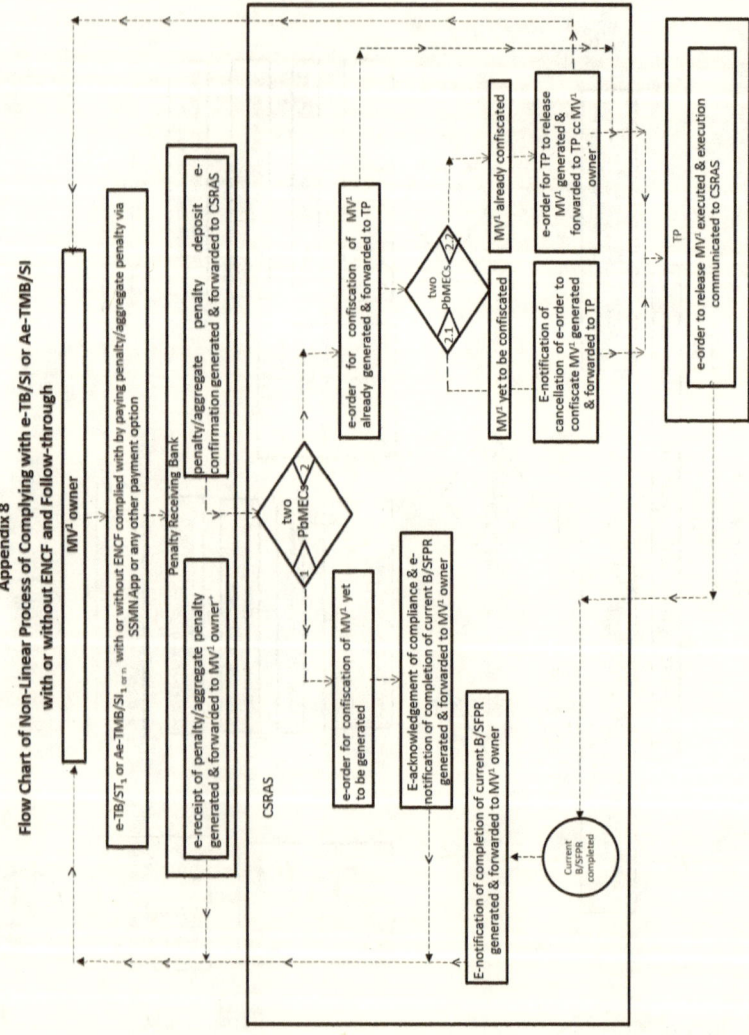

# INDEX

$3_{TC} + 6_{NC}$, 17-20, 22-27
360-degree profile, 42, 44-45
accidents, x, 130-131, 144-149
Aggregate e-Ticked for Multiple Bypassing/Speeding Instances (Ae-TMB/SI), 139-143
agriculture, 5, 17, 49
Ahya and Sheth, 38
Ambani, Mukesh, 30
andragogy, 48
Anti-Poverty Ministry, 41
Antilia, 30
Automatic Data Processing Module (ADPM), 133, 135-138
Ayushman Bharat Yojana, 17
Balakrishnan, Pulapre, 38
Bhagavad Gita, 115
Bhagwati, Jagdish, 35
Brahmaputra, 129
B/SIDS, 138-142

Bypassing Instance (BI), 137
Bypassing Instance Data Set (BIDS), 137
Bypassing/Speeding File Processing Rounds (B/SFPR), 138-143, 148
capital, v, x, 19, 28-29, 36-37, 39-46, 49, 51-54, 56, 59-60, 62, 66, 88-91, 95-97, 103, 123
carbon-emitting items, 125-127, 129
census, 30-31, 128
Central Statistical Organisation, 3
Central System for Real-time Action against Speeding (CSRAS), 131-132, 136-138, 140-143, 148
Chidambaram, P, 107
China, vii, 36-39, 63-64, 90-100, 104, 123

## Index

concept of economical piety, v, x, 112, 120-121

consumption, 1-3, 5-6, 10-11, 13-14, 39, 60, 95, 102, 107, 109, 119, 123, 125, 144, 148

Consumer Price Index (New Series) (CPI(NS)), 4, 12

Corporate Social Responsibility (CSR), 70, 91-92

Credit Suisse's *Global Wealth Databook*, 39

Criminal Reformation Programme, 75, 78-79, 83-84, 96

current account deficit, 95, 106

DALYs (Disability-Adjusted Life Years), 100

*dakhina*, 115

debt-to-GDP ratio, 63-64

deities, 112-114, 116, 118-120, 125-127, 129

*Delivering Road Safety in India*, 146

demonetization, 107

Digital Anti-Speeding Code Enforcement Ecosystem (DACE Ecosystem), xiv, 131-133, 138, 142-150

Digital Speed Limit Map (DSLM), 133-138, 148-149

direct beneficiary, 46-46, 48-49, 51-54, 58-67

discipline, 71-72, 84-85, 88

double-averaging, 7

dropout rate, 68

*Economic Times*, 146

economy, vii, xi, 29, 35, 38, 40-41, 55, 59, 61-63, 66-68, 88, 91, 95, 106, 108, 110, 123, 146

eligible persons, 44, 51, 58, 61, 63-64

Ema Keithel Lairembi, 117

Emoinu *Eratpa*, 114, 129

Escalating Non-Compliance Fine (ENCF), 140-143

e-Ticket for Bypassing/Speeding Instance (e-TB/SI), 139-143

excess-income-based monthly instalment, 54

exchange rate, 100, 148

Expert Group to Review the Methodology for Estimation of Poverty, 5

extravagant practices, 112-113, 120, 126

Faster Ride Mode (FRM), 134

Ganges, viii, 129

general education, 46, 48-50

Geolocation Code, 140, 143

Gini Coefficient, 39

## Index

globalization, 39

Global Positioning System (GPS), 131, 133, 135-138, 140, 144

gold, v, x, 38, 99-100, 104-111

Gold Monetization Scheme, 108

*Govardhan Puja*, 117

Government of India, xiii, 3, 5, 61, 89-90, 108, 110

Gross Domestic Product (GDP), 38-39, 63, 79, 100, 103, 105-106, 108, 110, 146

Hindu rituals, 127

hypothetical case, 6, 26, 59, 80-81, 95, 121

illiterate, 31, 75-78

IMSR-Backup Function (IMSR-BF), 136-137

incentive, 54, 65, 149-150

income share, 38-39, 52

India Brand Equity Foundation (IBEF), 104, 109

India Inc, 62, 91

Indian billionaires, 39

Indian culture, 108

Indian National Congress, 33, 64

*India's Gold Rush: Its Impact and Sustainability*, 108

Individual Motor Vehicle Folder (IMVF), 138-141

Informal Questionnaire Survey (IQS), 116-117

Information Exchange and Support System, 53

innumerate, 75-78

Integrated Fog/Rain Sensor (IFRS), 132-135

Integrated Milometer/Speedometer Reader (IMSR), 132-133, 135-137

Intensive Vocational and General Education Programme (IVGEP), 46, 48-53, 59-60

jail, 69, 72, 74-76, 84-86, 89-92, 94-95, 97, 139

Jaitley, Arun, 31

Jan Dhan Yojana, 17

*Janmashtami*, 129

jewellery, 39, 104, 106-107, 109-111, 128

calories, 5, 7-9

Knowles, Malcolm, 48

*Laibak Katpa*, 113

Lainingthou Sanamahi, 113-114

Lakshmi, xiv, 118, 121-124, 129

*Lamta Thangja*, 114

Lanjouw, P, 39

law of supply and demand, 66

Left Wing Extremism, 28
Leimarel Sidabi, 113-114
liberalization, 39
Literacy and Numeracy Programme, 46, 49, 51, 57, 75-76, 78, 96, 103
Maya, 119, 125
Meitei, 113-114, 116, 118, 126
Menon, Anjana, 146
MGNREGA, 35, 60, 63, 123
minimum income level, 54
minimum level, 1-2, 14, 16, 19, 22, 26, 54
Ministry of Coal, xiii
Ministry of Statistics and Programme Implementation, 3
Ministry of Skill Development and Entrepreneurship, 90
Ministry of Road Transport and Highways, 130
Modern Skill Education Centres (MSEC), 89-90
Modi, Narendra, 63
Modi, Nirav, 30
Money Value (MV), 24
Motor Vehicle (MV), 139-144, 149
Multiple Networks Access Subscriber Identification Module (MNASIM), 132-133
multiplier, 64, 95, 105
Murgai, R, 39
National Accounts Statistics (NAS), 2-3
National Bureau of Statistics of China, 36
National Crime Record Bureau, 75, 88, 91
National Democratic Alliance (NDA), 56, 63
National Food Security Act (NFSA), x, 8, 17, 126
National Infrastructure Pipeline, 63
National Sample Survey (NSS), 2-3, 37, 115
National Sample Survey Office (NSSO), 3, 5
National Skill Development Corporation, 89
National Skill Qualification Framework, 90
Nongda Lairen Pakhangba, 113
Nyuntam Aay Yojana (NYAY), 64-65
Panagariya, Arvind, 35
Penalty Receiving Bank (PRB), 132, 142-143
Piketty, Thomas, 51
Planning Commission, 5, 35

population, v, vii, x, 2-3, 21-22, 28-31, 35-36, 38-39, 42, 44, 52, 55-56, 63, 68-69, 72, 75-76, 87, 90-91, 93, 95-97, 100-103, 106, 108-110, 112, 127

Possible but Mutually Exclusive Cases (PbMEC), 139-140, 142

Possible but Mutually Exclusive Subcases (PbMES), 139-141, 143

*potsem jadu*, 124-125

poverty line, v, x, 1-3, 5-6, 12-18, 21-23, 26, 36, 110

Purchasing Power Parity (PPP), 2

Pradhan Mantri Awaas Yojana, 17

Pradhan Mantri Kaushal Vikas Yojana, 89

Pradhan Mantri Ujjwala Yojana, 6

primitive existence, 14

prison, v, ix-x, 34, 55, 68-69, 71-77, 82, 84, 90, 97, 116, 128

prisoners, 69, 71-72, 74-97

privatization, 39

production unit, 89-94, 97

psychological technique, 81

Rangarajan Committee, 3, 12, 30

Ravallion, Martin, 3

reformation, x, 71, 73, 75, 77-79, 83-84, 96-97, 160

Rehabilitation, 96-97

religion, 18, 27, 105, 112-113, 119, 121, 126, 129

$r > g$, 51

right, ii, 17, 37-38, 47, 60, 74-75, 77

righteousness, 120

*Rising Inequality: A Cause for Concern?*, 39

*Road to Perdition*, 146

S3, 22-23, 25-27

Sanamahism, 113

Santosh Mitra Square Committee, 127

Saraswati, 121

savings, 16, 19-20, 24, 60, 94, 108, 122-123

skill education, 71, 89, 94, 97

Socio Economic and Caste Census (SECC), 31, 34

Speeding Data Capturing Process (SDCP), 135-136

speeding, v, x-xi, 135-139, 144-145, 147-150

Speeding Instance Data Set (SIDS), 136

Speeding Instance (SI), 135-136, 139, 147

Speed Limit Breach (SLB), 134-135

Speed Limit Unbreach (SLU), 135-137

Smart Speeding Monitor-cum-Notifier (SSMN), 131-135, 137-138, 142-143, 147-149

SSMN App, 132-133, 137-138, 142

starvation, 25, 35, 55

*Statesman*, 146-147

Strategy for Eradication of Poverty through Intensive Development of Human Capital and Democratic Redistribution of Physical Capital - SEP(IDHC&DRPC), 40-42, 44-46, 52-55, 58-68

subsidy, ix, 34-35

Sundaram and Suresh, 3

tailor-made plan, 45, 52

tax-to-GDP ratio, 63

temple, 112, 114, 125-129

Tendulkar Committee, 2-3, 5, 12, 29-30

Tendulkar methodology, 30, 36

textile sector, 49, 90, 94

*Third Global Ministerial Conference on Road Safety*, 146

*Times of India*, 130-131

Topalova, P, 38

trade deficit, 108

traditional criteria, 16

Traffic Police (TP), 131, 140-143, 147-148

transformation, 58, 63, 97, 100, 104

United Nations Economics and Social Commission for Asia and the Pacific (UNESCAP), 146

*Vasudhaiva Kutumbakam*, 29, 82

*Vishwakarma Puja*, 117

vocational education, 46, 49

wealth, 38-40, 68, 122, 124, 128

World Bank, 2, 9, 35-36, 39, 146-147, 149

World Development Indicators, 36

World Gold Council, 99, 106-107

*World Inequality Report 2018*, vii, 38-39, 52

*World Wealth and Income Database*, 39

*yoo*, 124-125

www.ingramcontent.com/pod-product-compliance
Lightning Source LLC
Chambersburg PA
CBHW020910180526
45163CB00007B/2689

www.ingramcontent.com/pod-product-compliance
Lightning Source LLC
Chambersburg PA
CBHW020910180526
45163CB00007B/2689